Making the most of Hardy Perennials

by Alan Toogood

Published 1980 by Floraprint Limited, Nottingham. Printed in England.

ISBN 0 903001 45 4 (cased edition)

Alan Toogood underwent his horticultural
training at the Royal Botanic Gardens, Kew, and
Brighton Parks and Gardens Department. This
was followed by a two-year studentship at the
Royal Horticultural Society's Garden, Wisley,
Surrey. He subsequently spent eight years as a
horticultural journalist. From 1972–79 he was a
lecturer at Merrist Wood Agricultural College,
Worplesdon, where he taught a wide range of
horticultural subjects. He has a great interest in
hardy plants of all kinds, including perennials.

Contents

An introduction to hardy perennials

Hardy perennials have been in and out of fashion for many years, but modern garden design demands them and so they are rapidly coming back into favour after a period of neglect.

During the nineteenth century and the early part of the twentieth, perennials were very much in vogue, often being displayed in their own borders (frequently twin borders backed by hedges, separated by a wide grass walk), especially in the gardens of large private houses.

During that period many of the plants needed a great deal of staking and tying and, due to their often vigorous spread, frequent division and replanting. As we moved into a period when intensive maintenance could no longer be afforded, and gardens were being made smaller, these fine herbaceous borders, as they were called, and perennials in general, went out of favour and so grew a preference for more labour-saving plants such as shrubs and conifers.

In recent years eminent plant breeders and nurserymen have introduced a wide range of very much improved perennials and these are becoming widely known and grown by discerning gardeners. Gone are the old problems such as excessive maintenance, for many modern perennials are self-supporting, although not necessarily of dwarf stature. These newcomers are generally more restrained in growth than many of their older relatives, so we no longer need be afraid of introducing to our gardens plants like solidago, which once had the reputation of virtually taking over borders. Modern cultivars of this perennial are often dwarf in habit and do not wander excessively under the soil.

Hardy perennials have so many uses that it is difficult to imagine modern planting schemes which do not have a good selection of them. So how do we make the most of these plants? Many small gardens rely on mixed borders for all-the-year-round colour and interest and perennials, together with shrubs, bulbs and other plants, play an important part in such a scheme.

Many gardeners, however, still wish to grow perennials on their own and a modern way of displaying them is in informal island beds set in a lawn or a paved area. All of the plants used could be self-supporting, so making maintenance much easier.

To achieve a pleasing display of perennials, and other plants, colours must be used carefully so that they contrast or blend well with each other. We do not want violent clashes of colour, for instance, as a garden is supposed to be a restful place. Therefore I have made suggestions on how to use colour effectively, and have also provided some ideas for special colour schemes, such as a red scheme and a green and white scheme.

Have you ever considered the texture of leaves of perennials? Some have woolly leaves while others may be prickly, shiny or crinkled. As you will see in the following pages it can be great fun contrasting these textures in a planting scheme. The same can be said of leaf and flower shapes — you can let your artistic flair run riot, combining, say, spiky foliage with rounded foliage, or plate-like flowers with dignified spikes.

Making the most of perennials includes choosing plants which are at home in those problem spots which most gardens seem to have — such as shade or an arid situation, so I have chosen a range of plants for these conditions.

If I were to omit grasses from this book I am sure I would receive a shower of protests — and rightly so, for the ornamental kinds are among the most exciting perennials available. What better subjects are there for contrasting with all kinds of plants, especially shrubs, and with architecture and paving? There are so many kinds to choose from — some have blue or grey foliage, others are variegated silver or gold and many have impressive plumes of flowers.

A trend in garden design is to hide the soil as much as possible and therefore I have recommended a selection of low growing ground cover perennials for this purpose. Growing plants in pots, tubs and other containers on patios and terraces is also fashionable and some of the perennials I have suggested for this purpose provide quite an exotic effect.

There are, as you can see, many ways in which perennials can contribute to the overall planting scheme in a garden. Apart from giving ideas on uses of plants, I have also selected a wide range of plants that I consider are among the best perennials available. Of course, to get the best from perennials one must treat them well and therefore I have rounded off the book with cultural hints.

Many perennials have flowers of distinctive shape, such as the spectacular eremurus hybrids. Those with pale flowers show up well against a dark background, such as a deep green hedge.

1. Never a dull moment

A popular way of growing plants today is in a mixed border which contains perennials, shrubs, roses and other hardy and half-hardy plants.

In my introductory notes I indicated the many uses of hardy perennials in modern garden design. But before considering the uses in this and other chapters I feel that the definition of the term hardy perennial should be clarified. The term hardy is clear enough — it means that the plant is suited to outdoor cultivation all the year round. However, in one or two instances throughout the book you will find that I have recommended plants which are not hardy in all parts of the country. Some can only be grown successfully in milder areas. In cold parts of the country, where hard winters are commonplace, these plants could be damaged or killed. But the majority of plants recommended will withstand winters in any part of the British Isles.

Perennial means that the plant lives for a number of years, producing new foliage and flowers each year. But some of the plants are rather short lived, dying after perhaps two or three years. I have indicated this where appropriate. But such plants are in the minority and most live for very many years. If they are lifted and divided regularly most of the plants can be kept indefinitely. Paeonias are among the longest-lived of all perennials, and I know of clumps that are over fifty years old and which have never been lifted and divided. Paeonias, in fact, dislike being moved.

Basically there are two types of hardy perennial. Firstly there are the herbaceous plants. These produce new shoots in the spring from the crown, which is really a cluster of dormant or over-wintering buds. These shoots, of course, produce foliage and flowers. In the autumn these shoots die down to ground level, and then they are of no further use to the plant. They will never again produce leaves and flowers. So the gardener cuts them down to ground level and discards them. The plant then rests over the winter as a dormant crown and when the weather starts to warm up in the spring the buds spring into life and produce new top growth. Of course, herbaceous plants are of no interest throughout the winter, unlike the other type of perennial — the evergreen perennial.

Evergreen perennials retain their foliage all the year round and many of them are indeed attractive in the winter. All we need do with these at the end of the season is to cut off any dead flower heads and leaves. There are many examples of evergreens in this book.

You may now be asking yourself what is the difference between a perennial and a shrub? All of the perennials, whether herbaceous or evergreen, are non-woody plants, whereas shrubs produce woody or hard stems. Admittedly there are a few plants which, although classified as perennials, look very much like shrubs, but I do not think the reader of this book need worry about these odd cases. Most of the plants I have recommended are definitely non-woody in habit and are, therefore, unmistakably perennials.

So now to the many uses of these plants. In this chapter I have considered the role of hardy perennials in a mixed border. A mixed border contains plants such as shrubs, small trees, conifers, hardy perennials, bulbs, roses, and maybe hardy annuals and half-hardy annuals and perennials. This is a popular way of growing plants, especially in the small gardens of today. No one any longer has the space to plant different kinds of plants in their own special borders, which was common practice in the past. In the last century you would commonly see shrub borders, herbaceous borders and annual borders, and very good they looked, too (judging by old photographs).

But a carefully planned mixed border can be just as colourful and interesting and the aim should be to have something of interest all the year round — with never a dull moment. Even a small border could have interest right the way through the year. For instance, in the winter there may be a hamamelis in flower and perhaps a group of *Erica carnea*. In the spring perhaps some bulbs and early perennials like *Helleborus orientalis*. For the summer there is a wealth of shrubs and perennials to choose from, while for autumn colour there are the perennial asters, for instance, and many shrubs with colourful berries and leaf tints.

Plants vary in their requirements — for instance, some like full sun

In a mixed border hardy perennials can often be effectively grouped with coloured-foliage shrubs. Here an orange hemerocallis has been planted next to a purple cotinus.

7

and others shade; some need a cool moist soil and others flourish in dry conditions. If you can possibly site the border so that part of it is shaded and part in full sun, then you will be able to successfully grow a wider range of plants. Of course, there is little you can do about the soil, so you will have to choose plants which are suited to the border. Very often there is little choice regarding the siting of the border so care will be needed in choosing plants suited to the conditions which it provides. If it is permanently shaded then choose only shade-loving plants — do not grow those that need plenty of sun. If the border is in full sun, then you may have difficulty in growing some shade-loving plants and therefore these should be avoided. All of this may sound very obvious, but it is amazing how many people try to grow plants in totally unsuitable conditions. I would say that this is due to the fact that the plants' requirements are not known. I hope my book will help in this respect. Before you buy a plant make sure you are able to provide the right conditions for it. Borders generally need a background of some kind to hold them together. This may be a wall or a fence, or perhaps a hedge. If you intend planting a hedge as a background then choose something which is fairly dark green, such as *Taxus baccata, Thuja plicata, Chamaecyparis lawsoniana* 'Green Hedger', *Fagus sylvatica, Carpinus betulus* or *x Cupressocyparis leylandii.*

The plants should be planted about 1m away from a background hedge to prevent competition from hedge roots. An established hedge makes heavy demands on food and water during the summer to the detriment of any plants which have been set too close. Also, if the plants are set too close to the

An attractive colour scheme has been created here with the pink *Dicentra formosa* 'Bountiful', a yellow oenothera and a background of blue aconitum.

hedge they may receive insufficient light and therefore will make etiolated growth and produce a poor flower display.

The background hedge, and also the border, should ideally face south so that they receive the maximum sun.

A mixed border generally needs a permanent framework and this can be formed with shrubs, conifers and perhaps small trees. In between and around these can be planted hardy perennials, bulbs, annuals etc.

If possible try to have a lawn in front of the border to set it off; or maybe a paved area or a path. Many plants go well with paving and in small gardens it is being used more and more instead of grass. The latter quickly becomes worn in a small area due to constant use, and after a time it can become thin and patchy and

look most unsightly.

In order that a mixed border looks really effective it is necessary to choose plants which go well together. To my mind one cannot simply grow any perennial with shrubs — the perennials need to be carefully chosen so that they complement the framework of shrubs and look natural and harmonious with their woody neighbours. One should aim for contrast in shape of foliage and flowers, and in colour and texture of foliage and flowers. Below I have given some suggestions of perennials that I find associate particularly well with shrubs.

Acanthus mollis latifolius will contrast well with many shrubs as it has deeply divided green leaves and spikes of purple and white flowers in the summer. I particularly like to plant it near to the purple-leafed cotinus

In the summer a mixed border can be very colourful, with half-hardy annuals, tender perennials such as dahlias and hardy perennials. This border, backed with shrubs, is enhanced by a well-kept lawn.

cultivars. These have rounded foliage so there is good contrast both in colour and shape. I have also seen acanthus used effectively with shrub roses, which are the best type to grow in a mixed border rather than the more formal hybrid teas and floribundas. Plant it with pink shrub roses and the effect will be superb. You can also use *Acanthus spinosus* in the same way — it has similar foliage and flowers to *A. mollis latifolius*.

There are many kinds of kniphofia to choose from, but all have grassy foliage (in some it is thin, and in others broad) and bold spikes of flowers in various colours such as orange, red, yellow and cream. Orange or red kniphofias make good companions for the purple cotinus or even purple-leafed berberis. But it is safe to say that these perennials will look well with most kinds of shrubs. The grassy foliage contrasts well with the broader leaves of many shrubs.

Cynara scolymus is a magnificent foliage plant as it has large greyish leaves which make a pleasing contrast with purple-leafed shrubs. I can also recommend it with shrub roses of all colours. Perhaps even better in the mixed border is *C. cardunculus* which has deeply divided silver-grey foliage — again an excellent foil for roses, particularly red or pink cultivars.

Helleborus orientalis flowers in the winter and early spring and therefore is ideal for combining with shrubs that bloom during this period. The flowers are of various colours such as white, pale pink, crimson and purple, and the handsome foliage is evergreen. I like to grow large groups of this helleborus around the base of such shrubs as *Cornus mas*, hamamelis, forsythia, *Cornus alba* cultivars, *Chimonanthus praecox*, *Viburnum*

farreri and *Garrya elliptica*. A pleasant picture is created if it is massed around *Prunus subhirtella* 'Autumnalis' or one of the spring-flowering ornamental cherries. Include also in this underplanting some carpets of *Erica carnea* cultivars, and complete the picture with some groups of *Galanthus nivalis*.

Helleborus orientalis is also most attractive when planted with shrub roses; it flowers well before the roses, making a colourful display while the roses are at their dullest. When the roses are in flower the helleborus provides a background of handsome foliage, in no way detracting from the beauty of the roses. If you grow hybrid tea and floribunda roses then again this helleborus can be recommended for planting among them.

The thistle-like echinops, such as *E. ritro* and *E. humilis* 'Taplow Blue', can be strongly recommended for a mixed border. The foliage is good and they have blue flowers in the summer. Excellent companions for the golden-leafed *Philadelphus coronarius* 'Aureus' or *Elaeagnus pungens* 'Maculata', and equally attractive with purple or coppery-leafed shrubs. Similar in a way to echinops are the eryngiums like *E. tripartitum*. These also have blue flowers and like the echinops they are globular in shape. Use this plant in the same way. In my garden I have *Eryngium tripartitum* planted next to a *Berberis x ottawensis* 'Superba' which has large, spoon-shaped, very deep purple leaves. The eryngium sends up its flower stems through the branches of the berberis, producing a very striking combination of colour and shape.

There are many hardy geraniums to choose from and many have a very long flowering period in the summer. They come in many shades of pink, blue, red and

white and the plants look completely at home when grown around many kinds of shrubs or trees. I consider them especially attractive when massed around shrub roses. In this instance you will have to choose geraniums with suitable colours so that they do not clash with the roses. For instance, plant a blue geranium under a yellow shrub rose, preferably a pale yellow rose. The blue geraniums also look good when planted with yellow *Potentilla fruticosa* cultivars. These shrubs also have a very long flowering period in the summer.

To my mind hemerocallis look most at home with woodland-type shrubs such as rhododendrons and azaleas. These perennials have strap-shaped foliage and a long succession of lily-like flowers in a wide range of colours. But do combine these plants with other kinds of shrubs, trying to create contrast in flower colour. There are also countless combinations you could try using coloured-foliage shrubs. For instance, a pale yellow hemerocallis would look well with purple foliage.

I have recommended a good range of hostas in Chapter Eight so I will not list here the many kinds available. Suffice it to say that no mixed border is complete without some of these luxuriant foliage plants. Their bold leaves look well with most kinds of shrubs and they make superb ground cover in the summer. In many gardens which are open to the public you will find hostas massed among rhododendrons, azaleas, camellias, pieris and similar woodland-type shrubs. The green and glaucous hostas make a good underplanting for tall shrub roses.

Ornamental grasses, like the hostas, are also virtually indispensable in the mixed border as their narrow foliage makes an excellent contrast with the broad leaves of shrubs. Some of the variegated and glaucous grasses look well with purple-leafed shrubs such as cotinus and some of the berberis. Use grasses with some of the large-leafed shrubs like *Fatsia japonica, Mahonia japonica* and *Viburnum rhytidophyllum*. Grow some of the dwarf tufted grasses with roses, particularly grasses with glaucous foliage. Cortaderia, with its large handsome plumes of flowers, makes a striking contrast with shrubs which are noted for autumn leaf colour.

Heleniums are popular on account of their showy daisy flowers in the summer, which combine well with plants which have spikes of flowers. They are excellent when cut for indoor decoration.

2. An island in the sun

The traditional method of displaying hardy perennials is in their own borders backed by a hedge. This is known as a herbaceous border and it was a feature of many gardens in the past. The herbaceous border has gone out of favour among private gardeners, mainly because it involves a great deal of labour to maintain it and because modern small gardens do not have the space to devote a whole border to one type of plant. One can still see herbaceous borders in some of the larger gardens open to the public and they certainly create a fine display. The height of the display is in the summer.

Chapter One deals with one of the most popular methods of displaying perennials in the modern small garden — in mixed borders. However, there are many gardeners who still wish to grow hardy perennials on their own. An excellent method of displaying them, and one which is steadily increasing in popularity, is in island beds. These beds can be as large or as small as you wish to make them and if plants are carefully chosen they can provide something of interest all the year round. It is generally recommended that labour-saving plants are grown in island beds — those that do not need supports and those which do not spread vigorously. In the traditional herbaceous border many tall plants are grown and these need adequate supports.

An island bed should ideally be made in an open position which receives plenty of sun, for the majority of perennials need these conditions if they are to grow and flower well. The ideal situation for a bed is in a lawn as there is no doubt that a green sward is the ideal background for the bright colours of the perennials. However the bed could also be made in a paved area as paving is generally a fairly neutral colour and would not detract from the beauty of the flowers. In fact many perennials are much enhanced when associated with paving. I would not recommend that you set a bed in an area which is paved with coloured slabs — choose those of a natural stone colour.

Ideally an island bed should be in a sheltered situation to prevent the plants being damaged by winds or gales. If possible try to have some form of wind protection on the windward side, such as a bed or a group of shrubs.

In most gardens there will be space for only one bed, but if you have a large garden then do consider having a group of beds — say a group of three with adequate space between them to walk. But whether you have one or several, do make sure that there is space to walk all round, for an island bed should be viewed from all sides.

Whereas the traditional herbaceous border was very formal, island beds are the complete opposite. Each bed should be of an irregular shape but it should not be fussy in outline, especially if in a lawn as it would make mowing difficult. The outline of the bed should be gently curving or sweeping and certainly you should be able to run the mower around the edge with ease.

It is difficult to say much about size of bed for this will depend on the size of your lawn or paved area. But I can give a few guidelines. For instance, if you have a large lawn or paved area then it would be absurd to have a very tiny bed for it would not look in proportion to the site. If there is plenty of space make a large bed, or group of beds. There is no doubt that one can create far more impact with a reasonably large bed, for then it is possible to grow each kind of plant in a bold group. I consider that the minimum size for any group of plants is 1 sq m, even in a small bed. Of course, if the bed is small then you will have to grow only a few different kinds of plants. But I can assure you that it is far better to grow fewer plants and to display them in bold groups. Very small groups, or even single specimens, of many kinds of plants in a bed only create an irritating spotty effect.

I will not say much about planning island beds in this chapter for I have given some guidelines on using colour effectively in Chapter Three. But I have a few hints on the arrangement of plants, apart from colour. It is logical to plant the tallest perennials in the middle of the bed, with the shortest plants around the edge, and the intermediates between the two. This is so that all plants can be seen properly. But do not stick too rigidly to this arrangement otherwise you will end up with a very regimented effect, which looks unnatural. Instead, extend a few groups of dwarf plants towards the centre of the bed, and an occasional group of a taller kind towards the edge of the bed. This will break up what would otherwise be uniform ranks of plants.

Some of the early-flowering plants are not very attractive when they have finished flowering, and this applies particularly to such kinds as irises, lupinus and *Papaver orientale* cultivars. Such plants should be positioned towards the centre of the bed so that they are obscured by other plants when

An island bed in the height of summer. Such a bed can be as large or as small as you wish to make it, and a lawn makes an ideal setting for the bright colours.

their flower display is over.

Aim to have plants which flower at the same time spread fairly evenly over the bed. For instance, do not group all the spring-flowering kinds together in one part of the bed but space them out so that there is something of interest in various parts of the bed. The same applies to plants which flower in the summer, autumn and winter. But, of course, I am not saying that you should not have groups of contrasting plants together for this is one of the exciting parts of plant arranging — grouping together plants which contrast well in colour, texture or shape. But even so one can still spread the interest over the entire bed.

The types of plants suited to island beds are those which are self-supporting — in other words, plants which do not require canes or sticks to hold up the stems. This does not imply that only dwarf or low-growing perennials are used as many medium and tall-growing plants have sufficiently strong stems to hold themselves upright without the need for artificial supports.

Also the plants chosen should have a long, or a reasonably long, flowering period. There is no room in such beds for plants which have only a fleeting display of blooms. I would also suggest growing only plants which are fairly restrained in their spread — you do not want any rampant growers otherwise you will be forever lifting and dividing to keep the plants in check and, of course, this adds to the annual maintenance of the beds. The idea is to cut down on maintenance as much as possible. The plants should also be adaptable with regard to soils — plants with special soil requirements are often a great deal of trouble to grow well. All of the plants which I have recommended here are trouble free. I have picked out some of the best plants available for providing colour and interest throughout the year and as you will see I have, for convenience, grouped them under their appropriate flowering seasons. This is a personal choice of plants which I have found to be very reliable and trouble free and is not intended to be a complete list of perennials which are suited to island beds — indeed, there are many more which could be listed. However, the lists form a good basis for a collection and the idea has been to show what is available for flowering during each of the four seasons.

Perennials for spring flowering

Dicentra — although these perennials can be grown in full sun they do, in fact, enjoy semi-shade and a cool moist soil. But in either situation they are easy plants to grow. The best-known species is *Dicentra spectabilis* which is one of the tallest at 60cm when in flower. It has red pendulous flowers which are heart shaped when in bud. The flowers are well set off by the ferny divided foliage. It looks especially attractive when grown with doronicums, which have yellow daisy-like flowers at the same time as dicentra. Another

Dicentra spectabilis flowers in the spring and enjoys semi-shade and a cool moist soil, although it will take full sun.

Doronicum 'Miss Mason' makes a good companion for dicentras. It flowers over a long period in the spring.

Epimediums are excellent for island beds. They form carpets of handsome foliage and produce dainty flowers in the spring.

variety I would not be without is *D. formosa* 'Bountiful' with purplish-crimson flowers. It grows to a height of about 45cm and has deeply divided ferny foliage which remains an attraction after flowering. *D. formosa* is also worth a place in the garden and it is similar except that the flowers are pinkish mauve.

Doronicum — the doronicums are essential perennials for island beds as they make a superb display with their yellow daisy flowers and they bloom over a long period. I have already mentioned that they make good companions for dicentras, and I also like to grow them with the blue *Pulmonaria angustifolia*. There are several excellent hybrids to choose from, like the well-known 'Miss Mason' which grows to 45cm in height. It will take partial shade but can also be grown in full sun. There is a double-flowered hybrid called 'Spring Beauty', of the same height. This really looks superb with blue pulmonarias.

Epimedium — I have listed some epimediums in Chapter Eight, which deals with shade, but these perennials can also be grown in a sunny position. They are low growing ground cover plants and form carpets of handsome foliage.

Any species can be used in island beds, but I particularly like *E. perralderanum* which has yellow flowers and large evergreen glossy leaves. When in flower it will be about 30cm in height and is therefore an ideal frontal plant. *E. x warleyense* is a hybrid with distinctive copper-red flowers on stems a little below 30cm.

Euphorbia — the species *E. epithymoides* (also known as *E. polychroma*) is, like the doronicums, another essential plant for the spring. When in flower it reaches a height of 45cm and the stems carry flat heads of brilliant greenish-yellow bracts. The

15

actual flowers are insignificant. These heads remain in good condition for many weeks. The plant is very neat in habit, forming a bushy specimen. Excellent when planted with dicentras or with blue pulmonarias. It can be grown in partial shade or in full sun.

Pulmonaria — the rough leafed ground cover plant *P. angustifolia* has the most superb pure rich blue flowers which, as I have already indicated, contrast superbly with doronicums or with dicentras. The height of this plant when in flower is 23cm. For the best effect plant in really bold groups or drifts. Although it can be grown in full sun there is no doubt that it likes shade or semi-shade. There are several cultivars of this pulmonaria including 'Azurea' which is similar to the species.

Ranunculus — most people are very fond of the wild buttercups flowering in the spring and early summer on account of their rich yellow flowers. Of course, we would not have the British wild plants in our gardens as they are considered weeds, but I cannot praise too highly the alpine species *Ranunculus gramineus*. This has most attractive greyish-green grassy foliage and typical buttercup flowers in abundance. It grows to a height of 20cm when in flower and makes a very neat compact plant.

Veronica — the veronicas are sun-loving plants and of easy culture provided soil drainage is good. There are many species and cultivars to choose from and most of them flower in the summer. An early-flowering species, producing its spikes of pale blue flowers in May or June, is *Veronica gentianoides*. When in flower it reaches a height of 45cm and is excellent for the edge of the bed, or perhaps a little further back.

Euphorbia epithymoides is an essential plant for the spring. The greenish-yellow bracts remain in good condition for many weeks.

Pulmonaria angustifolia 'Azurea' contrasts superbly with doronicums.

Ranunculus gramineus is a neat plant ideal for an island bed.

16

Perennials for summer flowering

This is the largest group of perennials — there is certainly no shortage of summer-flowering plants and, in fact, some people tend to concentrate too much on these to the exclusion of spring or autumn-flowering kinds. One needs to achieve a reasonable balance between spring, summer and autumn-flowering perennials.

Aquilegia — the long-spurred hybrid aquilegias are very popular but unfortunately they are not long lived and new plants should be regularly raised from seeds sown outdoors or in a cold frame in June. The plants will flower the following summer. The 'McKana Hybrids' are among the best as they have very large flowers in a wide range of colours and a spur of up to 10cm long behind each flower. Height when in bloom is about 1m. These aquilegias can be effectively planted with various other summer-flowering perennials like lupinus and irises.

Campanula — the campanulas thrive in shade or sun and in any reasonably fertile well-drained soil. *Campanula lactiflora* is a superb plant with large heads of lilac bell-shaped flowers and growing to about 1.2m in height. In windy areas provide supports. The cultivar 'Loddon Anna' has pink flowers and 'Prichard's Variety' is violet-blue. *C. persicifolia* has cup-shaped flowers on 1m high stems. The colour is lilac-blue. I much prefer the white form of this called 'Alba'.

Clematis — the herbaceous clematis prefer a chalky soil but this is not essential. *Clematis heracleifolia* grows to about 1m in height and produces small sweetly scented blue flowers. The form *davidiana* has deeper blue flowers.

Coreopsis — these are very easily grown plants which flower over a long period. One of my favourites

Campanulas, like *C. lactiflora* 'Prichard's Variety', flower in summer and thrive in sun or shade and a fertile well-drained soil.

Euphorbia griffithii 'Fireglow' flowers in summer and needs to be grown with a 'cool' grey-leafed or white-flowered perennial.

is *Coreopsis verticillata* 'Grandiflora' which forms neat fine-leafed bushes about 60cm high covered with bright yellow daisy flowers. The blooms are good for cutting. Try growing it with some of the erigerons, for instance, or perhaps with blue campanulas.

Erigeron — hybrid erigerons are generally grown for display in island beds and they have daisy-like flowers over a long period. Most are lowish plants and are therefore given a frontal position. Some recommended cultivars are: 'Charity', pink, 60cm;

'Foerster's Liebling', deep pink, 45cm; 'Dignity', violet, 45cm; 'Sincerity', light blue, 45cm and 'Darkest of All', violet-blue, 60cm.

Euphorbia — one of the most brilliant summer-flowering perennials is *Euphorbia griffithii* 'Fireglow' which has heads of brilliant orange bracts on 75cm high stems. This colour has to be used carefully and I particularly like to combine this euphorbia with a grey-foliage plant such as an artemisia. Also it goes well with white-flowered perennials such as gypsophila. It also looks superb

with *Phalaris arundinacea* 'Picta' or *Helictotrichon sempervirens*. These two grasses are described in Chapter Ten.

Gaillardia — these perennials with their large showy daisy flowers, are best grown in very well drained soils and full sun. They are generally short-lived perennials but new plants are easily raised from seeds sown in the open ground during May or June. I must admit that the stems are not completely self-supporting and they are best given a few twiggy hazel sticks to keep them

The summer-flowering gaillardias are easy to grow if they are given a very well drained soil and a position in full sun. Support the stems with a few twiggy hazel sticks.

upright. But apart from this the plants are no trouble and are easy to grow. The flowers are excellent for cutting. There are several good hybrids available such as 'Ipswich Beauty' with red, yellow-tipped petals; 'Croftway Yellow', pure yellow; 'Mandarin', deep orange and 'Wirral Flame', brownish-red petals tipped with yellow. All grow to about 75cm in height.

Gentiana — growing to 1m in height, *Gentiana asclepiadea* has the most beautiful pure blue flowers and graceful willow-like foliage. This plant prefers a deep moist soil with plenty of humus but it is adaptable and will even grow well on chalky soils. It likes shade but can also be grown in the sun. I also like the white form *G. a. alba*. These gentians flower in late summer and into early autumn.

Geranium — there are many to choose from but one probably cannot do better than grow the *Geranium endressii* forms as they have such a long flowering period. There is 'A.T. Johnson' with pale silvery-pink flowers, 'Rose Clair' in bright pink, 'Wargrave Pink' in bright salmon-pink and 'Claridge Druce' with bright magenta-pink blooms. *G. endressii* itself has bright pink flowers and seems to be always in bloom. These geraniums are robust plants, growing to about 60cm in height and making very good dense ground cover. Cultivation is easy and I consider that every bed should have at least one or two of these completely trouble free plants.

Geum — the geums have strong bright colours and certainly make a good display in the early summer. Grow them near the front or edge of the bed as they are low in stature, attaining about 45cm in height when in flower. Divide the plants every three years to keep them young and

Each flower of hemerocallis lasts for only one day, but the plants produce a long succession of them in the summer.

vigorous. There are several good plants to choose from such as *G. rivale* 'Leonard's Variety' with bell-shaped coppery-pink flowers — a most unusual colour among perennials. *G. x borisii* is a popular hybrid with large single orange flowers. There are some good strains of *G. chiloense (G. coccineum)* like 'Lady Strath-eden' with double pure yellow flowers, and 'Mrs. Bradshaw' in brilliant orange-red, also with double flowers.

Helenium — popular plants on account of their showy daisy flowers in yellow, red, orange or brown, which are also good for cutting. Group them with white flowers or perhaps with some groups of variegated grasses. We generally grow hybrids and most

of these have been derived from *H. autumnale* and *H. bigelovii*. Some of the taller cultivars may need a few twiggy sticks to support the stems, but the lower-growing ones are completely self-supporting. I can recommend 'Bruno', bronze-red, over 1m; 'Butterpat', yellow, almost 1m; 'The Bishop', yellow, 75cm; 'Mahogany', coppery crimson, 1m; 'Moerheim Beauty', flame red, 1m and 'Wyndley', copper-orange, 60cm.

Hemerocallis — these perennials have lily-like flowers and each one lasts for only one day, but the plants produce a long succession of blooms in the summer. There are quite a few species but most gardeners grow the hybrids. All have the most attractive grassy

Lythrum salicaria 'Firecandle' is useful on account of its bold spikes of flowers, which are self-supporting and produced in the summer.

A *Chrysanthemum maximum* cultivar (foreground) acts as a foil for the strong colour of the monarda (background).

foliage which looks particularly pleasing in the spring when it is emerging from the crown. There are literally hundreds of hybrids which have been bred both in Britain and the United States. Their height is in the region of 1m when the plants are in flower, but this will vary slightly according to the hybrid. I have made a selection of some of my favourites and these are as follows: 'Black Magic', deep reddish purple; 'Hyperion', pure yellow; 'Morocco Beauty', deep purple with a golden throat and yellow stripe along each petal and 'Pink Charm', rose-red.

Lythrum — although the lythrums prefer boggy soils they can be grown successfully in a bed provided the soil is reasonably moist. Then they will produce many spikes of brilliant flowers. *Lythrum salicaria* cultivars are good plants, such as the bright pink 'Robert' and the brilliant rose-red 'Firecandle' and 'The Beacon'. *L. virgatum* 'Rose Queen' and 'The Rocket' have pink flowers. Height of all of these varies slightly but is around the 1m mark, certainly no taller.

Monarda — these perennials have aromatic foliage and square stems with attractive spidery flowers at the top. They like plenty of sun but for best growth need a reasonably moist soil. It is usual to grow the cultivars of *Monarda didyma* which reach about 1m in height. The best-known cultivar is 'Cambridge Scarlet' with red flowers, but 'Croftway Pink' is also attractive with clear rose-pink blooms. The newer 'Adam' is cerise-red while 'Prairie Glow' is a good salmon-red shade.

Phlox — the border phloxes are cultivars of *Phlox paniculata* and there are many dozens to choose from. These perennials prefer a moist fertile soil containing plenty of humus. Avoid chalky soils or heavy clay types as growth will not be very good in these conditions. Mulch annually with organic matter. Phloxes suffer from eelworm which causes the stems and leaves to become twisted and contorted and the stems to split. There is no cure so affected plants should be dug up and burnt. However, new plants can be produced from root cuttings in December. The roots are not affected by eelworm and so healthy new plants should result. Do not plant new phloxes on the piece of ground from which affected plants were lifted, as they may become contaminated with eelworm. Division of old clumps is not satisfactory and new plants should be procured from root cuttings. Some of the rich red cultivars are rather weak growers and also some of the reds and scarlets are inclined to fade in hot sun. Height varies according to cultivar but is in the region of 60cm to 1m or a little over. There are so many cultivars available that I would advise readers to choose the colours they prefer. Colours available include shades of red and orange-scarlet; purple and magenta; shades of lavender, lilac, blue, pink, carmine and salmon and white. All have a heady fragrance.

Pyrethrum — the pyrethrums are excellent early-summer flowering perennials whose blooms are often used as cut flowers. The stems are on the weak side and therefore it is advisable to provide a few twiggy hazel sticks for support. The plants need a good fertile soil and must have very good drainage. Provide a position in full sun and lift and divide as

In early summer the daisy-like flowers of pyrethrums associate happily with lupinus cultivars and bearded irises. There are many cultivars, single and double, and the well-known 'Brenda' is shown here.

necessary immediately after flowering. These perennials have daisy-like flowers, either single or double, and they associate particularly happily with lupinus cultivars and bearded irises, both of which flower at the same time of year. Some of my favourite cultivars include 'Avalanche', single white; 'Brenda', single carmine; 'Eileen May Robinson', single pink; 'Kelway's Glorious', single blood red and 'Progression', double pink.

Salvia — an indispensable perennial is *Salvia superba* with masses of spikes carrying violet flowers over a very long period in the summer. Height is about 1m. It can be grown in any soil but best results are obtained on a reasonably fertile moist soil. There is a lower-growing bushier form called 'Lubeca' which reaches about 60cm in height. Even shorter at 45cm is 'East Friesland'. These salvias look particularly good with daisy-like flowers, such as pale yellow anthemis or white *Chrysanthemum maximum* cultivars. They also make a good contrast with yellow flat-headed achilleas.

Scabiosa — excellent plants for a fertile, well-drained, and preferably chalky soil in full sun. The flowers are good for cutting. Cultivars of *Scabiosa caucasica* are generally grown, and they attain 1m in height. The best known is 'Clive Greaves' with lavender-blue flowers. A good white one is 'Miss Willmott'. A very long succession of blooms is produced, especially on young plants. To keep stock young and vigorous divide the plants every two or three years in the spring.

Sidalcea — these perennials are certainly well worth growing and they are completely trouble free, given a reasonably fertile soil which is not too dry and a sunny spot. The flowers are large and showy and are produced on

Scabiosa, like *S. caucasica* 'Miss Willmott', are excellent for fertile, well-drained chalky soil in full sun. The flowers are good for cutting.

The hybrids of *Tradescantia virginiana* are popular perennials, easily grown, and they flower from mid-summer until the autumn.

The summer-flowering sidalceas are completely trouble free given a reasonably fertile soil which is not too dry, and a sunny spot.

Invaluable perennials for autumn flowering are cultivars of *Anemone hybrida,* also known as *A. japonica.* They like sun and tolerate chalky soils.

stems up to 1.2m high, although some cultivars attain only 75cm in height. Some good cultivars include 'Croftway Red' at 1m in height and rose-red in colour and 'Rose Queen' at over 1m and a good shade of rose-pink. At 75cm in height is 'Loveliness' which has pale pink flowers.

Tradescantia — the hybrids of *Tradescantia virginiana* are popular perennials and they flower from mid-summer until the autumn. They are easily grown in any reasonable soil in the sun and reach about 60cm in height. Some of my favourites are 'Osprey', white with a blue centre; 'J.C. Weguelin', pale blue; 'Purple Dome', purple; 'Iris Prichard', white with a blue centre; 'Isis', Oxford blue and 'Leonora', mid-blue. One problem with tradescantias is that the foliage, which is grassy, is rather untidy as it flops around.

Perennials for autumn flowering

Anemone — the pink flowers of *Anemone hybrida* are produced on 1.2m high stems in early autumn. This plant is also known as *A. japonica.* It likes full sun and a fairly moist soil, and it revels in my chalky soil. There are some good cultivars such as the semi-double white 'Louise Uhink'; the rose-pink semi-double 'Mont Rose' and the single pale pink 'September Charm'. These perennials are inclined to be invasive but they are such beautiful plants and have such a long flowering period that most gardeners happily tolerate this habit.

Aster — the asters are the essence of autumn and every bed must have some, preferably those of medium or dwarf stature to cut down on staking. *Aster acris* is a beautiful plant but it has such large heads of flowers on tall stems that rain and wind quickly flatten the plants unless well

Asters are the essence of autumn. The *novae-angliae* cultivars are tall but they have strong stems, so are trouble free.

An easy-going perennial for early-autumn flowering is *Lysimachia clethroides* which is noted for its unusual curved flower spikes.

supported. Instead go for the lower-growing *A. acris* 'Nanus' which reaches only 45cm in height. The domes of flowers are a pleasant shade of lavender-blue. I am very fond of the *A. novae-angliae* cultivars, particularly 'Harrington's Pink' which produces clear pink flowers on 1m high strong stems. Most people, though, grow the *A. novi-belgii* cultivars, of which there are many. To cut down on staking grow only the dwarf or medium growers. The following grow between 45cm and 1m in height: 'Audrey', mauve; 'Chequers', violet-purple; 'Gayborder Royal', purple and 'Winston Churchill', red. Dwarf cultivars at about 30–45cm in height include: 'Blue Bouquet', blue; 'Little Red Boy', red and 'Snowsprite', white. The *novi-belgii* types suffer from mildew, some more so than others, and therefore one should commence a spraying programme in the summer before the appearance of this crippling disease.

Spray regularly with a systemic fungicide such as benomyl. These asters also need regular division — either annually or every two years. Divide in the spring, replanting young shoots with some fibrous roots — small shoots resembling rooted cuttings are ideal. Plant them in bold groups, about 5cm apart each way.

Lysimachia — an excellent perennial for early autumn flowering is *Lysimachia clethroides* which grows to about 1m in height bearing curved spikes of greyish-white flowers. It is fairly spreading in habit, especially in moist soils which it prefers.

Schizostylis — unfortunately *Schizostylis coccinea* can only be grown in mild parts of the country as it comes from South Africa. Ideal conditions are any type of fertile soil provided there is ample moisture available in the summer;

full sun and a sheltered spot. Divide every few years, in the spring, for best results. The plant grows to 60cm in height and produces rich crimson flowers. Other colours are available, such as the crimson *S.c.* 'Major', the pale pink 'Mrs Hegarty' and the pale pink 'Viscountess Byng'.

Sedum — the sedums have fleshy succulent leaves and the flowers are a great attraction for butterflies. An indispensable one is *S. spectabile*, 45cm high, with flat heads of pink flowers. Two good cultivars of this are 'Brilliant' which is deeper pink, and 'Meteor', which is also deeper in colour. I must also mention 'Carmen' which is another good deep pink cultivar.

Solidago — do not go for the tall

Schizostylis coccinea 'Major' makes a brilliant autumn display.

rampant kinds or you will probably regret it — they are rather weed-like. Instead choose a modern cultivar such as 'Goldenmosa'. This grows to 75cm in height and bears sprays of golden-yellow flowers. The foliage is also very attractive as it is golden-green.

Stokesia — although considered a summer-flowering perennial, *Stokesia laevis* 'Blue Star' has a long flowering season and will still be producing blooms in October. It has light blue daisy flowers on stems 45cm in height. It is a highly recommended plant for island beds and is of easy culture.

Perennials for winter flowering

Helleborus — in the winter and early spring the helleborus are the main providers of colour and interest as far as perennials are concerned. *H. niger* is the well-known Christmas rose which produces white bowl-shaped blooms on 30cm high stems. It has leathery evergreen leaves which provide a good background for the flowers. Success with this plant is achieved if it is grown in a moist soil rich in

Sedums have fleshy leaves and the flowers are a great attraction for butterflies. Shown here is the popular *S. spectabile* 'Brilliant'.

25

The modern cultivars of solidago are far more restrained in height and spread than the weed-like older kinds. The sprays of golden flowers help to brighten a bed in the autumn.

humus and in shade. There are some good forms of this species, such as 'Potter's Wheel' with extra-large white flowers. *H. orientalis* flowers in the late winter and early spring, sending up 45cm stems carrying bowl-shaped flowers. These are of various colours and most of the plants we grow are hybrids. Colours include white, purple, crimson, pink, red and cream. Some are attractively spotted on the inside. The foliage is ever-green. Any soil is suitable and the plants prefer shade or partial shade. Similar to *H. orientalis* is *H. atrorubens* but it has de-ciduous leaves and is not quite so tall. The flowers are deep plum purple and are generally pro-duced in January. It has the same cultural requirements as *H. orientalis*.

Helleborus niger, the Christmas rose, is one of the few winter-flowering perennials. It likes a humus-rich soil and shade.

3. Be colour conscious

The flowers and foliage of hardy perennials come in many colours and plants should be arranged to ensure that colours associate happily with each other. We do not want any violent clashes of colour in our beds and borders as a garden is supposed to be a restful place. It is safe to say that the majority of colours found in plants happily blend or contrast with each other, but there are exceptions and these will be pointed out in due course.

The basic colour of a garden should be green. A common mistake is to use too much colour in gardens so that the overall picture becomes unrestful.

Some people have a flair for combining colours while others do not. For many people it is a case of trial and error so I hope that this chapter will make it easier for readers to make pleasing colour associations.

A common mistake is to use too much colour in our gardens so that the overall picture becomes unrestful. The basic colour of a garden should be green. There is no doubt in my mind that this is the most important colour and all too often it is sadly lacking. There is really no better setting for flower beds and borders than a pleasant green lawn which acts as a relief from the often bright colours of the plants. A hedge or groups of shrubs, used as a backing for a bed or border, also help to set off the bright colours of flowers. We should also introduce green to our beds and borders in the form of grasses, perhaps, or hostas, ferns and similar plants. There are many shades of green so the effect will not be monotonous. For example, there is light, medium and dark pure green. Then there are plants with foliage in yellowish green, greyish green, bluish green and bronzy green.

Handling strong colours

Strong colours are probably the most difficult to arrange effectively — pastel or pale colours are much easier to group together.

When we consider red and strong pink flowers there is one very good and simple rule which readers would be well advised to follow. Reds and pinks can be split into two — there are those which have yellow in their composition and others which have blue in their make-up. The rule is never group reds and pinks which have yellow in their composition with reds and pinks which have blue in their make-up. The effect will be an uneasy clash and

In this strong colour scheme *Salvia superba* contrasts happily with a yellow achillea. There is also good contrast in flower shape.

will never be satisfying to the gardener.

In the summer there are many perennials with strong yellow flowers, together with brilliant orange-reds, flames and salmons. These colours go well together but are ideally associated with, perhaps, some plants which have coppery foliage and others which are yellowish green in colour.

You will find that the crimsons, magentas, pure pinks and mauves go well together, and with these colours you could also include, without fear of discord, plants with lavender, blue and bluish-green flowers or foliage. Further-

more, you could introduce plants with pale yellow and white flowers, plus those with silver or grey foliage. If you wish to add coppery foliage then do so as this will contrast happily with all of these colours.

A few hints on using yellow flowers. Green does not act as a good foil for yellow-flowered plants as it does with other colours — you need to think of a better contrast — paler or stronger, whichever appeals most. For instance, creamy-white flowers make a very good foil for yellow-flowered plants. You could use *Artemisia lactiflora*

28

A daring grouping of strong colours, which nevertheless 'works' well: blue *Agapanthus* 'Headbourne Hybrids' and a brilliant *Lilium tigrinum* cultivar. This group would need plenty of green foliage in close proximity.

with large plumes of cream flowers, or *Aruncus sylvester* with creamy-white plumes, among yellow-flowered perennials such as achilleas and verbascums.

Alternatively use stronger colours with the yellows, such as blue flowers or even plants with greyish-blue foliage like some of the grasses and hostas. I am particularly fond of including blue delphiniums among groups of flat-headed yellow achilleas, such as *A.* 'Gold Plate'. Here we also have an excellent contrast in flower shape — spikes and flat heads. For the spring you could plant drifts of blue pulmonarias around groups of doronicums which have yellow daisy-like flowers. The attractive greenish-yellow heads of *Euphorbia sikkimensis* are further enhanced with the violet spikes of *Salvia superba.*

Over the years I have made notes of pleasing plant combinations, including groups of plants with strong colours. It is appropriate to give some examples here and all the plants are, of course, hardy perennials. *Salvia superba* has strong violet flowers and these contrast effectively with the creamy daisies of *Anthemis tinctoria* 'Wargrave Variety', or the flat sulphur-yellow heads of *Achillea x taygetea*. This salvia has also been used effectively with *Chrysanthemum maximum* cultivars which have white daisy flowers.

Euphorbia griffithii 'Fireglow' has the most brilliant orange flowers which look most effective when combined with a grey-foliage plant such as an artemisia. In a mixed border a good effect is created if this euphorbia is planted near to the silver-leafed small tree *Pyrus salicifolia* 'Pendula'. 'Fireglow' also looks good when planted with white-flowered perennials like gypsophila, or with

ornamental grasses like the green and white striped *Phalaris arundinacea* 'Picta' or the bluish *Helictotrichon sempervirens.*

Some of the bright cultivars of *Phlox paniculata,* such as those with red or orange flowers, also benefit from the foil of phalaris, or even the grey-leafed *Anaphalis triplinervis.* Gypsophila, with clouds of white flowers, is also an excellent companion for the brightly coloured phloxes.

I like to see purple flowers grown with red and blue kinds. Here we are using the two colours which make up purple. For instance, purple phloxes could be grouped with red-flowered monarda and blue delphiniums.

Coming back to the violet *Salvia superba,* I have seen it grown very effectively with one of the red-flowered herbaceous potentillas.

Brilliant vermilion flowers could prove difficult and I am thinking here of *Lychnis chalcedonica* which is such a popular plant — no doubt on account of its colour. I have seen it grown with (yet again) *Salvia superba* and *Chrysanthemum maximum* cultivars. This is a marvellous combination: there is also good contrast in flower shape. This is a fairly safe scheme, but why not try this lychnis with the sulphur-yellow *Achillea x taygetea* and *Salvia superba?* Again a good contrast in shape as well as colour.

This achillea is also a good companion for *Geranium sanguineum.* The flowers of this perennial are deep magenta which is not the easiest colour to use. Other perennials can also be found in this colour. So try them with a sulphur-yellow plant and I am sure you will be pleased with the result.

A really superb, but simple, combination which I saw in a garden some years ago consisted of *Stachys macrantha,* which has

masses of deep rosy-mauve flowers in the summer, and *Alchemilla mollis,* a very well-known perennial with mounds of lime-green flowers. Both are low-growing plants which make good ground cover in the summer. A final hint for strong colours. If you want to play it safe remember that you can separate plants which are in danger of clashing with white-flowered plants such as gypsophilas, white phloxes, white *Chrysanthemum maximum* cultivars or white campanulas. Or you could use grey or silver foliage plants, or grasses — green and white striped or glaucous.

Making the best use of pastel colours

All pale and pastel colours, including white and off-white, are far easier to arrange than strong colours. But again, when using the pinks, remember to keep those which have yellow in their composition separate from pinks which have blue in their make-up. I am particularly fond of pale or pastel colours, mainly because they show up well in the fading evening light. White and pale yellow flowers show up particularly well. This adds to the attraction of a garden; after all, during the summer the garden should be used in the evening. To my mind there is nothing more pleasant than to sit in the garden on a warm, still summer's evening. Plants which I find show up particularly well include the white campanulas and phloxes and the pale yellow oenotheras.

Pastel colours are so useful for separating very strong colours and they also contrast well with strong colours. For instance, you could use pale pink flowers for separating red-flowered perennials, such as border carnations. Pale blue looks very good next to deep blue, a combination that could be used with delphiniums,

Pale pink flowers, such as this *Malva moschata,* can be used to separate red-flowered perennials.

for instance. Mauve-flowered perennials are very useful for placing between deep blues and purples, for instance with asters.

An illusion of distance

Colours can be used to create an illusion of distance and this is often desirable in the small gardens of today. Let us suppose, for instance, that your garden has a border, one end of which is close to the house and the other end is further away. At the far end of the border (the end furthest from the house) you could grow mainly plants with grey or pale blue flowers or foliage, thus creating the illusion of distance. It is these plants which create this illusion. The part of the border nearest to the house could be planted with subjects which have strong colours, so enhancing the illusion. We are only copying nature to some extent when we use this idea: the next time you are in the open country take a look at the distant trees — due to the distance they appear greyish or bluish, while the trees near to you are much stronger in colour. This idea can be applied to any planting scheme, not necessarily to a border. A group of shrubs and perennials with greyish or bluish colouration could be planted, say, in a far corner of your garden to create an illusion of distance, while plants nearer to the house could be of stronger colours.

Pale blue looks good next to deep blue, a combination that has been used here with delphiniums.

4. Special effects

In Chapter Three I discussed the uses of colour in fairly general terms so here I would like to suggest some rather more specialised plant groupings — creating special colour schemes by grouping together plants which have the same flower or foliage colour, or using just a few different colours in the one group.

For instance, you could have a red scheme, or a silver and pink, green and white, or a yellow scheme. I find this a very exciting way of displaying plants and it is a pity that so few amateur gardeners try such schemes in their own gardens.

Specialised colour schemes can certainly be seen in some of the large gardens which are open to the public, such as the famous red borders at Hidcote in Gloucestershire. There is also a green and white scheme at this garden. Admittedly these schemes are on a large scale and, of course, most people would not wish to devote an entire border or large bed to just a few colours. But there is no reason why you should not have a small bed or the odd corner of the garden devoted to a special colour scheme. Of course, it does not have to be a permanent feature, for it could be changed every three years or so when the plants, anyway, will no doubt need lifting and dividing. That is the beauty of hardy perennials — schemes can be changed frequently without any major upheaval, as is often the case with shrubs and more permanent plants.

But, on the other hand, there is no need to stick only to

A pink rhododendron effectively combined with a silver-leafed trailing perennial.

perennials in a special colour scheme: it could be a mixed planting of perennials, shrubs, bulbs and bedding plants.

You can certainly make use of coloured foliage in these special schemes, both the foliage of perennials and shrubs and ideally various types of plants should be used wherever possible.

A red scheme

I have already said that there is a good example of a red scheme at Hidcote. Actually the plants in these borders are not just red, but other colours have been used as well, such as orange and purple.

These borders are mixed; in other words, they contain plants other than just hardy perennials. The display starts in the spring when the red tulips come into flower together with red polyanthus. Then in the summer

there are red dahlias which are, of course, tender perennials and these are not planted out until all risk of frost is over in late May or early June. Permanent occupants of the borders are red roses and I would suggest that shrub roses are a good choice rather than the more formal hybrid teas, although the less formal floribundas could be used effectively. Do not forget that climbing roses could be trained up pillars to give height to the border. Contrasting with the dahlias and roses are the stately spires of purple delphiniums. *Rheum palmatum* is also used and this is a perennial. The best form of this is 'Atrosanguineum' with large deeply cut leaves which are reddish in colour, the young foliage being particularly brilliant. The flowers are brilliant red and are carried on 2m high stems in the summer, so place this plant towards the back of the bed or border. 'Bowles' Crimson' is similar and can also be recommended.

Purple-leafed shrubs are also used at Hidcote. Some good examples would be *Corylus maxima* 'Purpurea', *Cotinus coggygria* 'Foliis Purpureis' and *Berberis x ottawensis* 'Superba' or 'Purpurea'.

There are bold groups of *Salvia superba*, a perennial with spikes of violet flowers which are produced over a very long period in the summer and early autumn. These are the plants used a

The silvery-grey foliage of lavender makes an attractive foil for this bold group of golden-yellow *Coreopsis verticillata*. The coreopsis shows up well against the dark background.

Hidcote but, of course, there are other hardy perennials that could be included in a red scheme. You could use the red or orange cultivars of *Papaver orientale* which bloom in the early summer. But place them behind a more attractive plant so that their foliage is hidden after they have flowered, for it is not very appealing. Then there is the brilliant vermilion *Lychnis chalcedonica* and the red or orange lupins. Many of the cultivars of *Phlox paniculata* come in red or orange shades and these would make a superb show in the summer. A good ground cover subject for this scheme is *Ajuga reptans* 'Atropurpurea' which has purple foliage. For the front of the scheme one could plant red border carnations or pinks and some of the red geums. *Euphorbia griffithii*, preferably in the form 'Fireglow', is useful as it has brilliant orange flowers. Why not include an orange kniphofia with bold spikes of flowers and grassy foliage, such as *K. galpinii*?

For the autumn there are many cultivars of aster that you could use: there are many shades of red and purple from which to choose. Use dwarf cultivars for the front of the scheme and those of intermediate height further back. I would not recommend the very tall kinds as they need adequate staking to support the stems.

So why not try a red scheme? It creates a very warm and cheerful display and it is not so over-powering as it may seem. But do remember what I said in Chapter Three about using reds: those which have some yellow in their composition should not be placed next to those which have some blue in their composition.

A green and white scheme
Now for something cooler — a green and white scheme. There is

no doubt that this is more restful and is particularly welcome during the very hot days of summer. On the other hand, a red scheme very much brightens the garden on dull days!

The basis of a green and white group could be *Alchemilla mollis* which has mounds of lime-green flowers in the summer which are produced over a very long period. It is a low-growing perennial which makes very good ground cover in the summer. The lush, light green hairy leaves are an attraction in themselves.

Other shades of green, and also white, should be provided with several of the hostas and I have recommended a good selection of these in Chapter Eight. Although they like some shade they can also be grown in the sun provided they are kept moist in dry periods. Their large leaves contrast with other perennials and produce a very luxuriant effect.

Do not forget some of the ornamental grasses with leaves in various shades of green, or maybe striped green and white. A good selection will be found in Chapter Ten. For example, I would use *Phalaris arundinacea* 'Picta' with green and white striped foliage, *Festuca glauca* with glaucous leaves, and the bluish *Helictotrichon sempervirens*. Also the variegated *Molinia coerulea* 'Variegata'. You will find other good grasses in that chapter.

There are various white-flowered perennials that could be included, such as *Gypsophila paniculata* which has clouds of tiny white flowers in the summer. I am very fond of white campanulas and there are several from which to choose. There is *Campanula latifolia* 'Alba' with large pendulous white bells carried on tall stems in the summer. Another good tall one is *C. persicifolia*

'Snowdrift'. Use some white cultivars of *Phlox paniculata* such as 'Rembrandt' and 'White Admiral'.

I generally like a green and white scheme alongside a patio or sitting-out area, particularly because the white flowers show up well in the failing evening light and this adds to the attraction of this particular scheme.

A pink and silver scheme
Pink and silver schemes are more popular than most others, no doubt because they have been brought to the notice of the gardening public over the years by the late Mrs Desmond Underwood who had a nursery specialising in pink and silver plants. Over the years she staged many superb exhibits at the Chelsea Flower Show and at the fortnightly shows of the Royal Horticultural Society. She combined border pinks or dianthus with silver-foliage plants. Border carnations could also be used, of course — those cultivars with pink flowers.

So, the pink is provided by the summer-flowering border pinks and carnations or dianthus, in varying shades. There are so many cultivars to choose from that it is rather pointless just compiling long lists of them: choose those that appeal to you. Modern cultivars are very good and reliable.

So I would like to concentrate on silver-foliage perennials to grow with the dianthus. I use the term 'silver' rather loosely, for some of the plants have grey foliage.

Remember that all of these plants, including the dianthus, like a well-drained soil and full sun. The dianthus also appreciate a chalky or alkaline soil, although this is not essential and this scheme can be successful in acid soils.

Stachys lanata 'Silver Carpet' is a

A 'cool' green and white scheme is very restful, and particularly welcome during the very hot days of summer. Here are grouped green and white hostas, plus rodgersias, hederas and ferns.

plant that immediately springs to mind for this scheme. It is also known as *S. olympica* 'Silver Carpet'. This is a non-flowering form and is one of the best silver-leafed ground cover plants available. It has very woolly leaves which are evergreen, although they do become rather bedraggled in a wet winter.

There are several anaphalis which should be included, like *A. triplinervis* with greyish leaves and white everlasting flowers in the summer. Height is about 38cm. *A. cinnamomea* is also known as *A. yedoensis* and attains about 60cm in height. It has white felted stems and broad green leaves which are white felted below. It has flat heads of white everlasting flowers during the summer.

The artemisias are among the best plants for our purpose. I like *A. stelleriana* which grows to 60cm in height and produces grey-white foliage which is ever-green in mild parts of the country. It has tiny yellow flowers in the summer but these do not detract from the usefulness of this plant in our silver and pink scheme. *A. ludoviciana* 'Silver Queen' reaches 1m in height and has plenty of deeply cut grey foliage. *A. ludoviciana* itself is about 30cm taller with willowy grey-white foliage and tiny grey-white flowers in July and August. *A. absinthium* 'Lambrook Silver' has much-divided grey foliage and grows to 75cm in height. The tiny flowers are grey. This is one of Margery Fish's selections, another being 'Lambrook Giant' which is taller.

Lychnis coronaria has grey leaves rather like grey flannel and in the summer the 1m tall stems carry reddish-purple flowers. If possible for our scheme try to obtain the rather scarce white-flowered form called *L.c.* 'Alba'. These are short-lived perennials but they

sow themselves freely so you will never be without young plants. *Ballota pseudodictamnus* is a shrubby-looking plant whose leaves are covered with white wool and it grows to about 60cm in height. It may not be all that hardy in very cold areas but it is easily raised from softwood or semi-ripe cuttings rooted in a cold frame or greenhouse.

This is a restful scheme which I hope you will try provided you have the required conditions of good soil drainage and plenty of sun.

A yellow scheme

Something more unusual is a yellow scheme which can create a very bright sunny spot in a garden. There are many perennials to choose from and many of them have daisy-like flowers. You could also use yellow-leafed shrubs to form a permanent framework, like *Philadelphus coronarius* 'Aureus', *Corylus avellana* 'Aurea' or *Sambucus racemosa* 'Plumosa Aurea'.

As well as using yellow-flowered perennials you should also introduce cream flowers to this scheme to prevent the yellow from becoming overpowering.

Some suitable yellow-flowered perennials include various achilleas. *A. x taygetea* has light yellow blooms on 60cm high stems; *A.* 'Coronation Gold' is deep bright yellow and 1m in height; and *A.* 'Moonshine' produces pale yellow flowers on 60cm tall stems. They flower in the summer and all have flat heads of flowers which contrast very well with the tall spikes of yellow verbascums. Try *V.* 'Gainsborough' which is just over 1m in height. These are not long-lived plants and should be propagated regularly from root cuttings in December, rooting them in a cold frame or greenhouse. *V. vernale* is a true perennial with

2m tall spikes of vivid yellow blooms. The large basal leaves are very attractive and make good ground cover.

Cream-flowered perennials which can be included in the scheme include *Artemisia lactiflora* with large plumes of flowers which reach a height of 1.2m, and *Aruncus sylvester* of similar height and with plumes of creamy-white flowers. I particularly like to see the aruncus planted next to *Euphorbia sikkimensis*, a 1.2m tall perennial with flat heads of greenish-yellow flowers and red bracts.

Green does not make a good contrast with yellow flowers but you might like to try some of the grey-foliage plants which I recommended under pink and silver schemes. Grey and yellow is most pleasing and indeed you will find that some of the yellow-flowered perennials have grey foliage, like some of the verbascums and achilleas.

A yellow scheme can be a pleasant change, then, and what is more it will show up well in the fading evening light — some yellow flowers can become almost luminous in the dusk. A yellow scheme needs placing in front of a dark background so that the flowers really show up. Use, perhaps, shrubs with very dark green foliage like *Taxus baccata* or *Buxus sempervirens*.

I hope that these ideas tempt readers to try some special colour schemes. Remember that if you are not satisfied with the result you can always lift the plants and try something different. Also try some schemes of your own to see the effects you achieve. You will find it great fun arranging and rearranging plants until you have a scheme which really pleases you. To my mind a garden should not be static but there should always be something new in the way of plant combinations and groupings.

5. Leaves to be touched

A subject which is too rarely considered in relation to hardy perennials is leaf texture, and how to make use of leaf textures in planting schemes. The dictionary definition of texture, is 'The arrangement of threads in a woven fabric; the disposition of the constituent parts of any structure or material'. Texture, then, is something that can be seen, often aesthetically pleasing; and generally something that can be touched, not infrequently with a satisfying feel about it. The constituent parts of leaves are the microscopic cells which together make up each leaf. The arrangement of these cells results in a variety of textures on the leaf surfaces: for instance, some plants, like *Stachys lanata*, have very woolly or hairy leaves and others, such as *Acanthus spinosus*, are prickly or spiny. Then there are shiny or smooth leaves as in some of the bergenias, and crinkled or corrugated foliage which is the distinctive characteristic of the veratrums. All of these are distinctive textures — readily seen and felt. We can use them in many ways when creating planting schemes.

The way in which I like to use these plants is to group together several with very different leaf textures so that a dramatic contrast is created. A particularly pleasing combination is woolly and shiny foliage. For the woolly texture try the silvery grey *Stachys lanata* which is a low-growing ground cover plant. I recommend the cultivar 'Silver Carpet' which does not produce the purple-pink flowers of the

Stachys lanata has very woolly or hairy leaves which contrast superbly with the large, rounded, smooth, shiny leaves of bergenias.

species. I am not particularly attracted by the flowers, although some people will consider them a bonus. The leaves are evergreen although they can become rather tatty in a wet winter. Another suggestion is *Ballota pseudodictamnus* with white woolly leaves, but regrettably these become green as they age. Also the plant must be grown in very well-drained soil and may be damaged or killed in severe frosts. Either or both of these plants make a superb contrast with bergenias which have large rounded evergreen leaves. These are leathery in texture and generally smooth and shiny. A good selection of bergenias will be found in Chapter Eleven.

Prickly or spiny foliage and smooth leaves associate part-

Ballota pseudodictamnus has white woolly leaves which later turn green.

cularly well. I am fond of
Acanthus spinosus whose deeply
cut leaves have a spine at each
lobe. It is a stately plant with
purplish white flowers on 1.2m
high stems in late summer. Some
of the eryngiums have a prickly
appearance such as the rather
savage *E. agavifolium*. The 1.5m
long sword-like leaves have spines
along the edges. It sends up a 2m
high spike of white flowers. It is a
large plant, needing plenty of
space to develop, and in very
hard winters may be damaged or
killed. The leaves of *E. alpinum*
are deeply cut but not spiny,
although they give the appearance of being so. The metallic
blue thistle-like flower heads give
the appearance of being very
prickly but they are rather soft to
the touch. However, it is the
appearance that we are concerned with so this eryngium well
deserves a place in this chapter. It
flowers in late summer and will
gain a height of 1m or more. The
small rounded leaves of *E.
variifolium* form a pleasing rosette
and they are toothed and spiny.

An added attraction is their white
veining. The grey-blue flowers
have pale spiny collars and are
carried on 60cm high stems in
summer.

So what smooth-leafed plants can
we grow with the acanthus and
eryngiums? Something of similar
stature is needed and I would
suggest agapanthus. The species
A. campanulatus is one of the
hardiest and has attractive pale
blue flowers in late summer and
narrow strap-shaped grey-green
leaves.

The groups of plants that I have
mentioned need to be carefully
placed in the garden to further
enhance the effect. There is no
doubt in my mind that all of the
plants described, and those that I
shall mention later, are shown to
best advantage against stonework or brickwork. It may well be

The deeply cut leaves of *Acanthus spinosus* have a spine at each lobe. It is a stately plant, flowering in late summer.

The metallic blue thistle-like flowers of *Eryngium alpinum* give the appearance of being prickly but they are soft to the touch.

a wall constructed of natural stone or brick which of course gives a very solid background to these groups. Or the plants could be grouped close to a paved area, such as a terrace, patio or path. Again natural stone is the ideal choice, but you will find that the plants help very much to soften the appearance of artificial stone paving. These plants and brick paths seem to be made for each other and are an ideal combination in perhaps the cottage-style garden.

I have by no means exhausted the range of plants with interesting leaf textures so here are more perennials which are well worth trying and perhaps combining in groups of your choice. There seem to be more perennials with woolly leaves than with any other type of leaf texture. One of the woolliest must be *Verbascum bombyciferum*. It has large leaves, often over 30cm long and 20cm wide, and they are densely covered with white wool. The 2m high flower spike is also woolly and it bears bright yellow flowers in the summer. It is really biennial but I find that the plant persists in the garden as it sows itself, and seedlings spring up in various parts. The key to success with this plant is a well-drained soil and a position in full sun.

Unless the flower stems are removed *Salvia argentea* will also behave as a biennial. It is no great loss to remove them as they are rather drab, being white or a poor shade of pink. The plant is grown for its large leaves which are covered with silky silvery hairs. It is not one of the easiest plants to grow, requiring very good drainage and a sunny situation. It prefers an alkaline soil, although this is not so important as drainage.

Many of the helichrysums are of a shrubby nature but *H. plicatum* is more herbaceous in habit. It is

Some of the verbascums, which are noted for their stately flower spikes, have hairy leaves.

one of the hardier species with downy foliage but may be damaged during the winter in colder parts of the country. The leaves may reach a length of 10cm and they are covered with white down or wool. It grows to a height of about 45cm. This is another plant that I particularly like to grow with bergenias as they make a good contrast in foliage texture. The flowers of the bergenias, which are often pink or reddish, also look pleasing with the white foliage of this helichrysum. To succeed with this plant provide a well-drained soil, a sheltered position and full sun.

Lychnis coronaria has lanceolate white woolly leaves and I consider the foliage more attractive than the flowers. These are carried on 45cm stems and are a deep shade of magenta, a difficult colour to use effectively in a planting scheme. I prefer to grow the white-flowered form, *L.c.* 'Alba', as white seems to go well with any colour. Unfortunately the white form is not easy to obtain, but once you have secured a few plants you should have them for ever more as it sows itself very freely. This is just as well for it is a short-lived perennial, declining and eventually dying after a few years. I find that these plants grow very well in poor soils and they do not mind a very dry situation. The white form looks particularly attractive with a background of deep red brick so try if possible to grow it against a wall.

This, then is my choice of woolly leafed plants. There is another prickly plant that I must include, even though it is a biennial. This is *Onopordon acanthium*. Although biennial in habit it does sow itself very freely so you are never without young plants to replace those that have completed their life span. Indeed, I find it almost a weed in my garden — seedlings come up in the vegetable plot, in the lawn and fortunately in the beds and borders also. However it is no problem keeping it under control as unwanted seedlings are easily hoed off with the weeds. But I would not be without this impressive ornamental thistle: it is in fact

the Scottish thistle. It starts life as a silvery, very prickly rosette of foliage and in the second year the flower stems reach for the sky and may reach 2m in height, topped by purple thistle flowers. The large leaves are silvery and very prickly and the stems have broad wings. It is an ideal plant for the back of a group or border — but I always seem to make the mistake of growing it too near a path, so that in the second year, when the flower stem starts to branch, the path becomes impassable. You cannot simply brush this plant aside — it would be a most painful experience. This plant should really be sown where it is intended to grow it to maturity, as seedlings dislike transplanting due to their long taproot. A well-drained soil is needed and full sun. To show off the plants to best advantage provide them with a dark background such as a deep green hedge or a dark brown fence. One of the most successful groups I created was onopordon

planted near the purple-leafed *Cotinus coggygria* 'Foliis Purpureis', a very useful shrub for associating with many perennials. There are not, unfortunately, many perennials with shiny foliage. I have already mentioned the bergenias which are so useful for planting with woolly plants, but there are a few hostas with shiny leaves. *H. tardiflora* has narrow deep green shiny leaves and deep mauve flowers in the autumn. It is unfortunate that it is such a small plant and for best effect it should be planted in a fairly bold group. *H. lancifolia* has very shiny deep green leaves which are narrow and pointed. The deep lilac flowers appear in late summer on 45cm high stems. A larger plant is *H. ventricosa* with heart-shaped leaves of a deep shiny green and with wavy edges. The deep violet flowers are carried on 1m high stems in late summer. The hostas prefer a moist soil and are happy in light shade, which makes them difficult to grow with the other plants mentioned here. But a group of them is very pleasing in the vicinity of a patio or courtyard; their foliage and paving form a good combination.

Herbaceous perennials which have corrugated or ribbed leaves are few but among the best are veratrums. The most spectacular species are *V. album* and the rare *V. nigrum*. The foliage of these is similar: leaves up to 30cm in length and as much as 20cm across, and heavily ribbed or corrugated. The plants, if given suitable conditions, will eventually make large clumps. A deep fertile moist soil is needed and a shady position. Leave the plants undisturbed as they dislike being moved, but if you wish to divide the clumps then do so in the autumn because growth commences in early spring. They are such distinctive plants that a

Here the distinctively textured foliage of a golden juniper contrasts well with the smooth shiny leaves of bergenias.

41

Hosta 'Thomas Hogg' is a versatile plant: it has deeply veined leaves and the colour makes it suitable for green and white schemes. Here it contrasts well with the palmate leaves of rodgersia.

group of them in isolation is most pleasing. But I have seen them grown with agapanthus and also with liliums and the combination is dramatic. Veratrums are in the same family as agapanthus and liliums — the *Liliaceae*.

One of my favourite hostas has deeply ribbed leaves and this is *H. sieboldiana*. The large heart-shaped leaves are also of a superb colour — greyish blue. The flowers appear in summer and are white faintly flushed with lilac, but unfortunately they are carried on rather short stems and only just appear above the great clumps of foliage. *H. sieboldiana*, together with all of the hostas, luxuriates in moist soil and light shade. They can however be grown in full sun provided the soil is moisture retentive. This species is an excellent choice for associating with paving or stonework, such as a shady courtyard or patio. Do not be mean with the planting — have several plants together so that they form a really bold group.

It is an excellent plant for containers on a patio, terrace or in a courtyard and further details of this method of cultivation will be found in Chapter Twelve.

To make the most of leaf texture it is generally necessary to plant in bold groups — one is trying to make an impact and a single plant will not produce this. So many gardeners seem to be afraid of planting large groups because of the amount of space involved, but to my mind it is better to grow fewer kinds of plants and really make the most of them. A garden full of single plants of many kinds is rarely pleasing as nothing more than a spotty effect is created, which I find rather irritating. I must admit that it is a great temptation to grow a large selection but try to restrain yourself, especially if you have only a small garden.

Herbaceous perennials which have corrugated or ribbed leaves are few, but among the best are the veratrums. This one is the rare *V. nigrum*.

Geum x borisii has quite good foliage and is a trouble free plant for an island bed, flowering freely in early summer.

6. Consider the shape

Many hardy perennials have attractive and distinctively shaped leaves, flowers and even seed heads. These plants should be carefully displayed so that they show their particular features to best advantage. Some could be used as isolated specimens, say in a lawn or paved area, perhaps creating a focal point in a garden. Others can be used as a striking contrast to the house or some other architectural feature, while there are some which look particularly pleasing when planted near a water feature. Let us take a look at some of these plants and also consider possible uses in a garden.

Leaf shape

Plants with distinctive foliage often make very good lawn specimens or add an exotic touch when planted near a patio or in a courtyard. One can have great fun grouping together plants with different leaf shapes to create interesting contrasts.

Among the finest plants for use as lawn specimens are the rheums. One of my favourites is *Rheum palmatum* 'Atrosanguineum' whose large deeply cut leaves are bright red when they are produced in the spring. The huge flower spike, up to 2m in height, appears in early summer and carries panicles of crimson flowers, followed by attractive seed heads. *R.p.* 'Bowles' Crimson' is very similar. For best results the rheums need to be grown in a fairly deep, fertile, moist soil and in the sun.

The cynaras look particularly well near a paved area and can also be

Ligularia przewalskii has both distinctive flower spikes and foliage, and should be grown in moist soil. It flowers in June and July.

recommended for planting with shrubs in a mixed border. Good companions for them are purple-leafed cotinus or berberis. Many people would think of planting them only in the vegetable garden but to my mind their foliage is far too attractive to be hidden away behind the runner beans. The best planting time is spring and they should be given a well-drained soil and full sun. *Cynara cardunculus* has silver-grey, deeply divided leaves and in good growing conditions these may attain over 1m in length. In the summer 2m high grey stems are produced, topped by huge purple

Rheum palmatum, and its cultivars, has very bold foliage, making it an ideal specimen plant for a lawn or patio.

The foliage of *Cynara scolymus* looks particularly good near a paved area, or with shrubs in a mixed border.

thistle-like flowers. Its close relative, *C. scolymus,* also has large attractive leaves but they are not so grey as *C. cardunculus.* But the plant attains a similar height in the summer when it bears its blue thistle-like flowers. The flower heads are a gastronomic delight so will, no doubt, be harvested before they are fully open. However, I am recommending this plant for its foliage so the effect will not be ruined by gathering the flowers.

The rodgersias have large hand-shaped leaves which may be more than 30cm across. But they also bear attractive flowers in the summer which are something like those of astilbes. Ideal conditions include a moist soil and sun or partial shade. Some people plant them in the marshy ground beside a pool and indeed they flourish, and look most attractive, in such a setting. I must admit that I like to see them associated with modern architecture and also growing in a shingle or pebble-covered bed, which is becoming a popular way of displaying plants. Another very attractive way of displaying the rodgersias is in the light or dappled shade of a woodland garden. I have seen attractive groups of rodgersias and phormiums — a combination of palmate and sword-like foliage. In this instance you would need to grow the plants in the sun, and make sure the soil was sufficiently well-drained for the phormiums.

There are several species worth growing such as *Rodgersia pinnata* which, as the name suggests, has pinnate leaves. The pinkish flowers are carried on red stems in the summer. There is a much-improved form of this species called 'Superba' which has bronze foliage and clear pink flowers. This is the one I would recommend. *R. aesculifolia* has very large basal leaves each com-

45

posed of seven leaflets and they are tinted with bronze. The white flowers may be carried to a height of 1.2m. The leaves of *R. podophylla* have large cut lobes and are tinted with bronze when they first appear. The cream flowers are carried in drooping panicles and may reach a height of 1m. Then there is the very fine *R. tabularis* which has circular leaves up to 1m across and of a light shade of green. The astilbe-like white flowers are carried to a height of 1.5m.

The glaucous lobed leaves of *Macleaya cordata* should definitely not be hidden by other plants. It is a tall plant, 2m in height, but despite the height is self-supporting. The creamy-white flowers are carried in panicles during July and August. Use this plant as a specimen, perhaps in a lawn. If used in a shrub border (and it does contrast well with many shrubs) do make sure there are no plants in front of it as its attractive foliage is produced from ground level upwards.

Phormium tenax comes from New Zealand and I have found it to be hardy in all but the coldest parts of the country. Indeed, I find it a very adaptable plant: it will grow well in all kinds of well-drained soils and is suitable for coastal planting. It will flourish in areas with a polluted atmosphere. A position in full sun should be chosen to ensure the best growth. The evergreen sword-like leaves are greyish green and may reach a length of 3m. The reddish flowers appear in summer, often on stems up to 4.5m in height. I have already mentioned that phormiums are excellent for contrasting with other plants which have foliage of a different shape, such as the rodgersias. They make good lawn specimens and add a touch of the sub-tropical to a patio or terrace. There are a few good cultivars

46

Rodgersia pinnata has distinctive foliage, and is best grown in moist soil and in sun or partial shade.

The lobed leaves of *Macleaya cordata* should definitely not be hidden by other plants. Use this plant as a specimen, perhaps in a lawn.

such as *P.t.* 'Purpureum' with bronze-purple foliage which contrasts with grey-leafed plants. The leaves of *P.t.* 'Variegatum' are edged with cream, and those of *P.t.* 'Veitchii' are striped with pale yellow.

The dwarf *Eryngium bourgatii* attains a height of only 45cm and it has deeply cut glaucous leaves which are marked with greyish white. The blue summer flowers are surrounded with long spiny bracts. It is an easily grown plant, thriving in well-drained soil and a sunny position. It looks rather attractive at the front of a bed or border, especially if near a path or paved area.

The following four plants should ideally be planted near water to show them off to advantage. Indeed they need to be grown in the moist soil at the edge of a pool or stream. The first is a fern, *Osmunda regalis*, a rare British native found in boggy areas. It is probably our largest-growing fern, attaining a height of up to 2m. It eventually makes a huge clump of magnificent fronds, which are a fresh green in the spring and summer. Then in the autumn, as they die, they turn a rich golden-brown. Plant this fern so that it is in isolation — it needs no other plant to enhance the effect.

For owners of really large gardens there is the huge waterside plant *Gunnera manicata*. The massive lobed leaves may be up to 2m across and are carried on thick prickly stems. The leaves are rather coarse and bristly. The plant is often over 2m in height and has an even wider spread. The massive flower spikes are dull green and not particularly attractive. The plant comes from southern Brazil and therefore it could be damaged by frost in the winter if not protected. The usual method is to bend one or two of the leaves over the crown in the

There are several cultivars of *Phormium tenax,* like 'Sundowner' shown here. The sword-like leaves contrast well with many other plants.

Osmunda regalis is a tall fern with magnificent fronds, and ideally should be grown at the edge of a pool or stream.

47

autumn and to pile a heap of bracken or straw over the top. Due to its rather tender nature it is best to plant gunnera in the spring.

The rhizomes of *Peltiphyllum peltatum* will ramify the soft wet soil at the edge of a pool or stream and bind it together, so preventing erosion. Sun or shade is acceptable. The roundish leaves may be 30cm or more across and appear after the light pink flowers in April.

Podophyllum emodi delights in moist soil, rich in humus, and partial shade. It has attractive lobed leaves and in the spring bears white or pale pink flowers singly on erect stems. The large red fruits are edible although the rest of the plant is poisonous. Maximum height is 45cm.

Flower shape

Many perennials have flowers of distinctive shape and I find it great fun to group together plants with different-shaped flowers. Try, for example, delphiniums, which have stately spikes of flowers, with some of the flat-headed achilleas. Or perhaps a group of eryngiums, which have globular flowers, with some daisy-like plants such as *Chrysanthemum maximum* cultivars. The combinations are endless, so let us have a look at some of the perennials which have distinctive flowers. Remember that they should be planted where they will show to best advantage.

There are many perennials which produce their flowers in spikes and probably among the most popular are the delphiniums, which often grow to over 2m in height and flower in the summer. Therefore each flower stem will need a bamboo cane for support. Main requirements are a fertile soil, good drainage and full sun. Plus slug pellets in the spring to protect the emerging shoots from slugs and snails. It is best to raise new plants every three to four years by taking basal cuttings in the spring: they should be about 7.5cm long and rooted in a cold frame. There are many named hybrids to choose from, in various shades of blue, and also mauve, purple, pink and white.

Lupinus Russell Strain has very fat spikes of flowers in a wide range of colours and gains a height of about 1m although some cultivars may grow slightly taller. But the stems are self-supporting. These plants do not grow well on chalky or limy soil and rather resent clay types. The ideal is a light soil, on the acid side, and well-drained. Renew plants regularly, as for delphiniums, and also protect from slugs and snails. To prolong the flowering period cut out dead flower spikes. The main flowering period is in June.

Liatris spicata produces its spikes of purplish flowers in late summer and autumn. The flowers start opening from the top of the spike. Provide a light soil if possible, but ensure sufficient moisture is available, and full sun. The flowers, incidentally, are especially good for cutting — and the removal of a few spikes often prolongs the flowering period.

Perennials which are best grown as isolated specimens, ideally in a lawn, to show them to advantage, are the kniphofias. They have attractive grassy foliage and stately flower spikes in the summer. It is essential to provide well-drained soil (they will tolerate very dry conditions) and a warm sunny position. To protect the crown from excessive winter wetness tie the leaves together in the autumn — rather like a wigwam. There are many kinds to choose from but among my favourites are *K. caulescens* with glaucous foliage and 1.2m spikes of light red flowers; *K. uvaria*, which is probably the most widely grown species, having orange-scarlet and yellow spikes of a similar height and *K. galpinii*, growing to under 1m and bearing orange flowers. There are several good named cultivars such as 'Bees' Lemon', 1m; 'Maid of Orleans', ivory, 1m and 'Royal Standard', red and yellow, 1m plus.

Digitalis are excellent for planting under trees in dry or moist soil. Probably the most sumptuous

Kniphofias are best grown as isolated specimens, ideally in a lawn, so that their stately flower spikes and grassy foliage show to advantage.

Rudbeckia fulgida 'Goldsturm' is a good example of a daisy-flowered perennial. It likes a well drained soil and sunny position.

spikes are produced by the 'Excelsior' hybrids which carry their flowers all round the stems and hold them horizontally. Colours range from white and cream, through pale yellow, to pale pink, rose-pink and purple, and the stems generally reach a height of 2m. This strain is biennial but plants sow themselves very freely. Some of the perennial species are interesting, like *D. ambigua* with pale yellow flowers on 75cm stems, and *D. x mertonensis* with flowers the colour of crushed strawberries. Height is 1m.

The giant eremurus are really spectacular and should be planted in a fertile, well-prepared soil, in a position where they will be protected from wind. The fleshy roots are very brittle. The 'Highdown' cultivars are to be recommended. They were raised by Sir Frederick Stern in his Sussex garden, which was created in a disused chalk pit. So if you have a

chalky soil the eremurus are among the plants you should be able to grow successfully. Some of the cultivars are 'Highdown Pink', pale pink; 'Highdown White' white; and 'Highdown Yellow', yellow. All grow to about 2m and flower in the summer.

For a moist border or waterside planting I can recommend *Ligularia przewalskii* which attains a height of 1.2m when in flower. The purplish stems carry yellow flowers in June and July and the handsome foliage is deeply cut.

Perennials with flat heads of flowers are particularly useful for associating with spikes — they provide a good contrast in shape. Probably the best-known plants are the achilleas such as *A.* 'Coronation Gold' and *A.* 'Gold Plate'. The first attains a height of about 1m and the second will grow to 1.2m. Both have golden-yellow flowers over a very long period from mid-summer on-

wards. I am also fond of *A.* 'Moonshine' with pale yellow flowers. It grows to a little over 60 cm in height and flowers in mid-summer. The foliage is silvery-grey. All of the achilleas like a well-drained soil and full sun — in fact, they are among the easiest plants to grow.

Sedum 'Autumn Joy' is reputed to be a hybrid between *S. telephium* and *S. spectabile* and it has bright salmon-pink flowers in large heads during late summer and autumn. It is one of the indispensable late-flowering perennials and as it grows to only 60cm in height is an ideal front-of-the-border plant.

Now we come to a large group of plants — those with daisy flowers. There are the rudbeckias with their cone-centred flowers, such as *R. deamii* with a black cone and bright yellow ray florets. It flowers from August until October and will reach 75cm in height. Then there is *R. fulgida*

'Goldsturm' which is similar but with larger flowers, and it is slightly shorter. The rudbeckias like a well-drained sunny position. The helianthus need the same conditions and, like rudbeckias, are easily grown. 'Capenoch Star' has single bright yellow flowers and will reach 2m in fertile soil. The flowers of 'Monarch' can attain 15cm in diameter and are a good golden-yellow shade. They are carried aloft on 2m high stems. Both plants flower in late summer and autumn. Some of the vigorous helianthus will need regularly lifting and dividing —this certainly applies to 'Monarch'.

The inulas thrive in any reasonable soil provided they are given full sun. I. magnifica is indeed a magnificent plant but it needs plenty of space — it will reach 2m in height and has a spread of about 1m. It has large rough foliage and brownish stems carrying bright yellow daisies. It has many uses — it looks good with shrubs (particularly with coppery or purple-leafed kinds), makes a handsome lawn specimen and looks particularly at home beside water.

Also best planted near water is Ligularia clivorum as it likes moist or boggy conditions. It is also known as L. dentata and has large heart-shaped leaves and large orange-rayed flowers in July and August. Height is 1.2m. A sunny position should be provided for best results.

The white daisy flowers of Chrysanthemum maximum are frequently seen in borders and they are produced in succession from mid-summer until well into the autumn. There is a particularly good cultivar in 'Everest' which has large flowers in abundance. It rarely needs supports and is completely trouble free, growing in any well-drained soil and full sun. It grows to about 1m in height. Even taller at 2m is C.

The large bowl-shaped blooms of *Papaver orientale* appear in early summer. This cultivar is the well-known 'Perry's White'.

uliginosum with large white flowers and a pale yellow centre. It is very late flowering, the blooms appearing in October.

Anthemis tinctoria cultivars flower throughout the summer and are especially good for cutting. They thrive in any soil, provided drainage is good, and in full sun. The two most trouble free are 'Mrs. Buxton' and 'Wargrave', both with pale yellow daisies, and growing to about 75cm in height.

An unusual colour in daisy flowers is crimson-purple and here we have Echinacea purpurea which blooms in the summer. It grows to 1m in height and is no trouble provided the soil does not become excessively dry. As with most of the daisy-type perennials full sun is needed. My final choice in this group is Heliopsis patula which attains 1.5m in height and bears bright yellow frilled flowers during the

summer. It is quite a vigorous grower but does not make a nuisance of itself.

Some perennials have large bowl-shaped blooms and those that immediately come to mind are the hybrid paeonias: the cultivars of P. lactiflora or the Chinese paeonia. These are among the longest-lived of all perennials and once planted should be left undisturbed. Conditions required are a good deep fertile soil, plenty of space in which to grow, and an annual mulch of organic matter. The best planting time is in the autumn and care should be taken not to damage the roots as they are very brittle. The young shoots must be set about 5cm below soil level. Unfortunately paeonias do not flower over a very long period but they are among the early perennials, producing their breath-taking display in early summer. There are so many cultivars available

The spectacular bowl-shaped flowers of *Paeonia lactiflora* cultivars appear in early summer. These are among the longest lived of all perennials and once planted should be left undisturbed.

that it is best if gardeners choose those that most appeal. There are many shades of pink, red, crimson, white, primrose and cream. The most popular cultivars are the doubles or semi-doubles, but there are also single cultivars available.

Papaver orientale cultivars flower in early summer and often have blooms up to 15cm across. They are not exactly trouble free as generally they need staking and after flowering their foliage becomes decidedly tatty and needs to be hidden. Therefore the plants are best set behind a later-flowering perennial, so that after the papavers have finished their display the frontal plants will grow up and hide the foliage. They are easy plants to grow provided the soil does no become too wet in the winter, in which case the roots may rot Some good cultivars include 'Marcus Perry', orange-scarlet 'Perry's White' and 'Salmon Glow', double salmon. None grows more than 1m in height.

Perennials with globular flowers are useful for contrasting with other shapes, such as plumes o

Perennials with globular flowers, like *Echinops ritro,* are useful for contrasting with other shapes, such as plumes or spikes. Echinops have stiff self-supporting stems and flower in summer.

pikes. One of my favourites is *Eryngium tripartitum* which has large heads bearing many small steel-blue flowers from mid-summer until well into autumn. Although easily grown, I find that it does need some form of support as the flower heads become top-heavy. Height is never more than 1m and I particularly like to grow this perennial with purple-leafed shrubs such as berberis or cotinus cultivars. It grows particularly well on chalky soils. In a way rather similar are the echinops, such as *E. ritro* with deep blue globes on 1.2 m high stems in summer. *E. humilis* 'Taplow Blue' is even taller at 2m and has bright blue flowers. They both have stiff, self-supporting stems.

A favourite group of perennials are the cultivars of *Trollius x cultorum* which thrive in a moisture-retentive soil and sunny position. They flower in May or June depending on the cultivar and some of the best include 'Earliest of All', lemon-yellow; 'Goldquelle', buttercup yellow and 'Orange Princess', of the same colour. Height is 60cm.

Perennials with plume-like or feathery flowers make a good contrast with many plants. Cultivars of *Astilbe x arendsii* are particularly attractive when planted near the edge of water where they enjoy the moist soil. They can also be grown in a border provided the soil does not become dry. A little shade is also appreciated if possible in order to ensure a long flowering period. They flower in July and August. A mulch of organic matter is desirable, especially if the plants are being grown in a border. Some good cultivars include 'Cattleya', lilac-pink, 75cm high; 'Deutschland', white, 75cm and 'Red Sentinel', brick red, 75cm.

Given a good moist soil and partial shade *Aruncus sylvester*

Cultivars of *Astilbe x arendsii,* with plume-like flowers, are particularly attractive when planted near the edge of water – they enjoy moist soil.

will produce luxurious foliage and 2m high white plumes in June. Unfortunately it does not have a very long flowering period and the dead heads are best removed as they look unsightly. After flowering the foliage remains attractive.

The clouds of tiny white flowers of *Gypsophila paniculata* are so useful for toning down many of the border plants with strong or difficult colours. They appear in the summer. There are several cultivars, including the popular 'Bristol Fairy' with double flowers. The single cultivars are longer-lived plants than the doubles. Gypsophila is not too fussy as regards soil and is especially recommended for chalky types. Height of growth when in flower is approximately 1m and often the plants benefit from a little support in the form of twiggy hazel sticks as the flower heads can become top-heavy, especially when wet.

Seed heads

Seed heads should not be ignored and several perennials have, in fact, some very attractive seed heads. *Physalis franchetii* has bright orange-red seed pods shaped like lanterns. Growth is very vigorous and plants should therefore be given plenty of space. These perennials will thrive in any soil and in sun or shade. *P. franchetii* grows to about 75cm in height but 'Gigantea' will reach about 1m. Both have rather floppy stems so will need the supports of twiggy hazel sticks.

Then there is the striking *Phytolacca americana* which, although a rather coarse plant, is nevertheless worth growing for its autumn spikes of shiny maroon berries. It reaches a height of 1.2m. It is probably best grown in a shrub border where it makes a fine display with the help of shrubs with autumn leaf tints. It will grow in sun or shade and prefers a moist soil. The plant is

The 'lanterns' of physalis make a bright display. Plants will thrive in any soil and in sun or shade.

The seeds of *Iris foetidissima* persist for many weeks.

poisonous so I would not recommend it for households with small children.

The evergreen *Iris foetidissima* has lilac flowers in early summer but the main attraction is the seed heads. When the pods open bright orange seeds are exposed and they persist for many weeks in the autumn. It grows to about 60cm in height and will thrive in any soil and in sun or shade. It is a particularly good perennial for chalky soils. This iris probably looks most at home when grown under trees.

7. Scented flowers and foliage

Scent, fragrance or perfume, call it what you will, certainly adds another dimension to a garden. Most people like fragrant flowers and foliage and, of course, they are especially appreciated by blind people. Generally fragrant plants attract bees, butterflies and other insects, so creating further interest in our planting schemes.

It is unfortunate that there are few hardy perennials with scented flowers, compared with shrubs. But there are some and I have listed the best-known kinds further on in this chapter. There seem to be more hardy perennials which have fragrant foliage. As with most plants which have this characteristic, it is necessary first to pinch or brush the leaves in order to release the fragrance. Again I have listed a good range of hardy perennials with scented leaves further on in this chapter. Plants which possess scent, whether in the flowers or in the foliage, should be sited quite carefully in the garden so that their characteristic can be easily appreciated. For instance, scented plants should ideally be planted alongside a path so that they can be sniffed or pinched as one walks by. There is nothing more annoying than having to step into a border or bed in order to appreciate the scent of some plant. By constantly doing this, of course, you pan down the soil and invariably damage other plants in the process.

Another good place for scented plants is alongside a patio or

You either like the foliage scent of *Nepeta x faassenii* or you loathe it. It is an easy-going perennial, given good drainage.

some other area used for sitting. If this area is very sheltered the scent from plants will be all the better. In a more open, windy aspect a great deal of flower scent goes unnoticed.

Let us now have a look at a selection of fragrant hardy perennials.

Scented flowers

There is one perennial which springs to mind immediately and this is *Convallaria majalis*. The white bell-shaped flowers of this dwarf plant have the most delicious scent and it is difficult to

tear yourself away. It is a pity this is such a low-growing plant for you have to get down on hands and knees in order to appreciate it. On the other hand, many people prefer to cut some flowers and bring them indoors — they last well in water. The flowers show up well against the pale green foliage. There is a variety called 'Fortin's Giant' which has larger flowers, again highly fragrant. Perhaps you prefer a pink variety, in which case try 'Rosea'. Conditions required for successful growth are shade and a good supply of moisture.

The dianthus (border pinks and carnations) are another obvious choice, many of them possessing a very strong clove fragrance. Plant along the edge of a path, as they are low-growing plants and make a good edging. They like an alkaline soil, so if you have a chalky soil they should do well. Provide a spot in full sun.

Some of the hostas have scented flowers such as *H. plantaginea*. The pure white flowers, which appear in late summer, have a similar scent to convallaria. The large rounded yellowish-green leaves of this hosta provide a further attraction.

The lupinus, especially the popular Russell Strain, have quite a subtle scent which is not to everyone's liking: when grown in a massed display the scent becomes rather heady.

Some of the oenotheras have scented flowers and at the same time are excellent and reliable border plants. What they like in the way of conditions are a well-drained soil but at the same time adequate moisture in dry weather and a position that receives plenty of sun. *O. speciosa* has white flowers which turn pink, but they have only a slight fragrance — which is better than nothing. These are produced from May to September on 45cm high stems. *O. biennis* is, as the name suggests, a biennial, so it has to be renewed each year from seeds. It may well sow itself in your garden. It has large yellow flowers which are pleasantly scented and they open in the evening. They are produced on 1m high stems from July to September.

Paeonia lactiflora has pure white fragrant flowers and is a most beautiful plant. The double or Chinese paeonias originated from this species and many of these are also well scented, such as 'Duchesse de Nemours', cream;

Many of the dianthus possess a very strong clove fragrance. Plant along the edge of a path as they make a good low edging.

'Felix Crousse', crimson and 'Lady Alexandra Duff', blush pink. Paeonias are quite easy to grow and they will thrive in most soils provided they are prepared well before planting by deeply digging and manuring. These perennials do not like to be disturbed once planted: simply give a mulch of well-rotted manure in the autumn each year and lightly prick this into the surface in the spring.

Finally, all of the varieties of *Phlox paniculata* are fragrant — indeed, they give off a very heady scent, especially if the garden is sheltered from the wind.

Scented foliage

Anthemis cupaniana is one of my favourite daisy flowers and it forms mats of very aromatic foliage. The scent is, to my mind, reminiscent of nepeta.

Many of the artemisias have aromatic foliage and they are grown mainly on account of their foliage which, in many, is a silver or grey colour. Like the anthemis, they are excellent plants for growing in dryish soils and in full sun. The fragrant *Artemisia abrotanum* is a well-loved perennial and is seen in many old cottage gardens. *A. lactiflora* also has highly fragrant foliage, and attractive plumes of creamy-white flowers in the late summer and early autumn. *A. ludoviciana* is a striking plant with white woolly leaves which are aromatic. These are among my favourite artemisias — there are others and in fact it is a big genus.

very much like the highly aromatic foliage of *Calamintha nepetoides*. This plant forms compact low bushes and is admirable for edging a path or a patio. The lavender flowers appear from June to September. The scent is something like a combination of mint and nepeta, and is very pronounced when the foliage is pinched or rubbed. Provide full sun and good drainage for this easy-going perennial. Some of the geraniums have aromatic foliage and this is especially true of *G. macrorrhizum* which has pink flowers from spring to mid-summer, and the white form 'Album'. The

The many cultivars of *Phlox paniculata* are fragrant — indeed, they give off a very heady scent, especially if the garden is sheltered from the wind.

Monarda didyma cultivars have very aromatic leaves as well as being good flowering plants. This one is named 'Croftway Pink'.

long period, and reach 60-90cm in height.

You either like the smell of nepeta or you loath it. Many people must like it for it is a well-loved cottage-garden edging plant which has been grown for generations. There are several kinds but the best-known is *N. x faassenii* (commonly but wrongly known as *N. mussinii*). It forms carpets of grey foliage and has lavender-mauve flowers from spring to autumn. It is often grown on the tops of retaining walls, or down the edges of steps, as well as alongside garden paths and patios. A very easy-going plant, given good drainage and plenty of sun. Try one or two other nepetas such as *N. nervosa* with spikes of violet-blue flowers from July to September. Or there is 'Souvenir d'Andre Chaudron' with large tubular flowers in deep lavender-blue and greyish-green foliage. Both of these are low-growing plants.

Origanum vulgare 'Aurea' is a golden-green leafed form of a British native plant. It is an excellent perennial for edging as it attains only about 15cm in height. The foliage is highly aromatic when pinched or brushed with the hand. It is important to grow this perennial in the sunniest spot available and the soil must be gritty and well-drained.

The same conditions should be provided for the salvias which also have highly aromatic foliage. The varieties of *S. officinalis* have very aromatic as well as highly ornamental foliage. They make neat plants up to 60cm in height. There is the green and gold variegated 'Icterina', the purple-leafed 'Purpurascens' and the grey, white and pink 'Tricolor'. I find it best to prune these back regularly in the early spring each year to make sure the plants remain compact.

scent is really strong and distinctive and some people I know dislike it. But to others, including me, it is most pleasing. This is an excellent low-growing perennial which thrives in dry or moist soils and in full sun or partial shade. It makes very good ground cover if closely planted, as it is quite a vigorous grower.

I cannot leave out the menthas, although these are mainly culinary herbs. But there are one or two ornamental kinds which to my mind should be in every garden. *Mentha rotundifolia* 'Variegata' is a most attractive green and white variegated plant with a typical smell of mint. It is a rampant grower, especially if provided with a moist soil which it likes. It will grow in partial shade if necessary. This plant grows to about 30cm in height. Then there

is *M. x piperita* which is really a culinary herb, but it is well worth growing in the ornamental part of the garden for its peppermint-scented leaves. The purple flowers appear in late summer and are not unattractive. Height about 60cm. It requires the same conditions as *M. rotundifolia* 'Variegata'. There are many creeping and carpeting menthas but these are more suited to rock gardens than to beds and borders. Every bed or border should have monarda on account of its flowers. But there is a bonus in the highly aromatic leaves. Most people grow the varieties of *M. didyma* in various shades of pink, red and purple. Try also *M. fistulosa* 'Violacea Superba' with deep violet-purple flowers and, again, aromatic leaves. All of these flower in the summer for a

8. Shady spots

It is often thought that shade is a difficult situation in which to grow plants but this is certainly not so if suitable plants are chosen. Indeed, many perennials luxuriate in shade or semi-shade and to my mind some of the most beautiful planting schemes can be created in such conditions.

The types of plants chosen depends on the soil. In some gardens there is shade with dry soil, and in others shade with moist soil, so it is best if I consider these separately.

Candelabra primulas are a natural choice for a moist woodland garden. They flower in June and July.

Shade with moist soil

If you have shade or partial shade with moist soil then you will be able to grow some of the most beautiful and choice perennials available. There are many superb plants which demand these conditions, including a range of woodland plants. For instance, you could make an attractive planting with groups of the Candelabra primulas and meconopsis or blue poppies, all much enhanced by the luxuriant foliage of hostas and ferns. This type of planting scheme can be seen in many gardens open to the public in which there is light woodland, such as oak or birch woodland.

Of course, the gardens of most houses do not have woodland conditions, although it is possible to have a small woodland planting if you have a few trees which cast dappled shade. If you have a large enough garden there is no reason why you should not plant a group of suitable trees, such as *Betula pendula,* to create a mini-woodland. These trees grow very quickly and soon create the desired conditions.

Very often in suburban or town gardens there are shady corners, the shade being cast by buildings. Such situations are again ideal for the plants which I will describe later. So take a look around your garden to find a spot that is shady or partially shady and try a group of woodland-type plants.

Having decided on a suitable place for this scheme it may be necessary to prepare the soil before planting. Most of the plants that like shade with moist soil also appreciate plenty of humus in the soil — they like a moist cool root run. So when you are digging the ground prior to planting it is advisable to include a good quantity of peat or leaf-mould in the soil. Of course, leaf-mould is the natural choice for

Athyrium filix-femina is a superb fern for moist shade, but it can be grown in dryish soils. This is a cultivar, 'Corymbifera'.

The young unfurling fronds of dryopteris are quite spectacular in spring. This fern will grow in moist or dryish soils.

this scheme but peat is a good alternative. Shredded bark has come on the market in recent years and this is also suitable for digging into the soil.

After planting it is recommended that you permanently mulch the plants with leaf-mould, peat or shredded bark to prevent the soil drying out rapidly in dry weather and to keep the roots of the plants cool during the spring and summer.

Remember that there is no need to use only perennials in this scheme — you could form a 'framework' with woodland shrubs such as pieris, camellias, rhododendrons, hamamelis, halesias and kalmias, but bear in mind that they need acid or lime-free soil. The perennials can then be planted between and around these shrubs — ideally planting in drifts or bold groups of each type of plant. You could also include various bulbs such as liliums, fritillarias and endymions.

Although you have a moist soil remember that in very hot dry periods in the spring and summer the soil can still dry out, in which case the plants will suffer badly. Therefore it will be necessary to carry out regular and thorough watering during drought conditions.

As I mentioned earlier there is a good selection of plants to choose from for moist shady conditions, so now let us consider some of them.

I would like to start with ferns which produce a cool, luxuriant effect with their fronds, and which provide a pleasing foil for the flowers of primulas and meconopsis. *Athyrium filix-femina* is a British native plant which is generally found in moist places, although I must mention that it can be grown in dryish soils. The fronds are much divided, are an attractive fresh green and they die down in the autumn. They will

A fern which needs moisture, and which can even be grown beside a pool, is *Matteuccia struthiopteris* which resembles a giant shuttlecock in shape.

grow to 60 cm in height. This fern will reproduce itself from spores, provided you do not disturb the soil around the plants. Spores are the equivalent of seeds in the fern world and are found on the undersides of the fronds enclosed in sori or spore cases.

Dryopteris filix-mas is also a British native and grows to about 1m in height. Its fronds are also much divided and are evergreen in sheltered areas, although in other areas they will die down in the autumn. It is an extremely hardy fern and will, like athyrium, grow in moist or dryish soils. This fern will also reproduce itself from spores. There are many

forms of this fern with crested fronds, the best known being *D. filix-mas* 'Crispa'. It is lower growing than the species, reaching about 45cm in height.

A fern which definitely needs moisture, and which can even be grown beside a pool, is *Matteuccia struthiopteris*. This fern has a most unusual habit of growth — its fronds are carried in a formation which resembles a giant shuttlecock and they reach a height of about 1m, dying down in the winter. They are a pleasant fresh green in the spring but will not tolerate an exposed situation or a dry soil.

A very well-known British native

is *Phyllitis scolopendrium* which will grow virtually anywhere. However, there is no doubt that it makes the best growth in shade with a moist soil. It has long, bright green, tongue-shaped fronds which carry strings of spores on the undersides. The fronds are generally evergreen but by the end of the winter are decidedly tatty and I generally cut them off to make way for the new fronds. It grows to 45cm in height. There is a most attractive form with wavy fronds called *P. s.* 'Undulatum' which is well worth searching for.

Another native of Britain, and other parts of Europe, is *Polystichum aculeatum*. It has 60cm long, prettily divided, evergreen fronds which are yellowish green in the spring but darken and become shiny as the season progresses. *Polystichum setiferum* is also a native of Europe, including Britain, and is one of the most beautiful ferns available. It will grow to 60cm in height and the fronds are evergreen, looking good right through the winter. The fronds are dull green and are a beautiful sight when they are unfurling in the spring. This fern will grow well in dryish soils.

This, then, is my selection of ferns. These plants are regaining their popularity after a period of neglect. Ferns were very popular in the Victorian period, when they were often grown in ferneries — simply a collection of different kinds. After the Victorian period ferns went out of favour. But gardeners are now beginning to appreciate the value of these plants in all kinds of planting schemes.

Other foliage plants that we need in our scheme to act as a foil for the flowers are hostas. Actually these plants are quite adaptable as they will thrive in moist or dryish soils, in very dense or partial shade, and in full sun.

A very well-known British native fern is *Phyllitis scolopendrium* which will grow virtually anywhere, but best growth is made in moist shade.

One of the largest-leafed hostas is *H. sieboldiana elegans* which is a beautiful shade of blue-grey. It bears lilac-white flowers.

They will flower more freely in sun but in deep shade flowers will be sparse, but the foliage will be larger and more luxuriant. They are excellent plants for growing in the shade of a north wall. If you have a thin chalky soil it will be necessary to add plenty of organic matter before planting. I grow them quite successfully on my chalky soil but there is plenty of humus underneath them. One must protect hostas from slugs and snails as these pests will devour new shoots in the spring and also the fully expanded leaves in the summer. I use slug pellets based on methiocarb and find these very effective. It is necessary to put slug pellets round the plants before the new shoots start to appear in the spring, and then repeat the applications as necessary throughout the growing season.

Hostas produce lily-like flowers in the summer but most people would agree that it is the foliage which is the main attraction. The foliage dies down in the autumn but during the summer it makes excellent ground cover around shrubs and other plants. If you have the space hostas are best planted in bold groups so that you obtain a dense mass of foliage. Try not to plant hostas in frost pockets as the spring growth could be damaged by late-spring frosts. Otherwise these perennials are perfectly hardy and trouble free.

Hosta crispula has large leaves which are deep green with a broad white margin. The edges of the leaves are wavy. This is one of the best of the hostas with white-edged leaves. It is one of the earliest to flower, producing in early summer pale lilac trumpet-shaped blooms on 75 cm stems. H. 'Thomas Hogg' has smooth deep green leaves with a wide cream margin, and pale lilac trumpets on 60cm high stems in early summer. It is often confused with H. crispula but unlike that species has smooth leaves. It is a very well known and popular hybrid.

A very common but popular species is H. fortunei which has long pointed leaves in mid-green. It soon forms a dense clump up to 45cm in height. The flowers are pale lilac and carried on 75cm high stems. There are some excellent forms of this hosta, such as H.f. 'Albopicta' which forms clumps of broad leaves, these being bright yellow with a pale green edge when young. They become pale green with a deep green edge as they mature. The trumpet-shaped flowers on 75cm high stems are pale lavender and appear in mid-summer. A superb form is H.f. 'Aurea' with completely yellow leaves in the spring and early summer. As they age they fade to green. The height is about 60cm but unfortunately I have never found this form to be very vigorous in habit and it needs planting in bold groups to produce a striking effect. H.f. 'Marginato-Alba' has mid-green leaves which are broadly edged with white. It is a superb form and one of the best of the white-edged hostas. The lilac flowers are produced in summer and are carried on 75cm high stems. H.f. 'Obscura Marginata' is rather a peculiar name and readers may be more familiar with this plant if I say that it was previously known as 'Yellow Edge'. The old name was far more appropriate for this hosta has its leaves broadly edged with creamy yellow. This edge does not fade and it remains attractive right through until the autumn.

One of the largest-leafed hostas is H. sieboldiana — the leaves are often 30cm wide and over 30cm long. They may be deep greyish green or bluish. It forms a large clump of foliage and in the summer white flowers on rather short stems (75cm in height) appear just above the foliage. Probably an even better plant is H. s. elegans with leaves of the same size but a beautiful shade of blue-grey. They are very deeply veined which adds to their attraction. The trumpet-shaped flowers are lilac-white and are carried on 75cm high stems, appearing just above the foliage. Undulate or twisted leaves is one of the characteristics of H. undulata. They are deep green and shiny and the centre of each leaf is creamy white. In late summer trumpet-shaped lilac flowers are produced on 45cm high stems. Overall this plant produces a very light-coloured effect. I would like now to turn to some plants which are grown for their flowers. The main flowering plants in our scheme must be primulas of various kinds. Among the earliest to flower is P. denticulata which sends up its globular lilac flower heads on thick stems from March to May. It grows to about 30cm in height and can be planted around the base of spring flowering shrubs. It is very easy to grow and quickly makes large clumps. There are forms in various colours, like P.d. 'Alba' which is white, and P.d. 'Prichard's Ruby' which is rich ruby red. It is interesting to note that this primula can be propagated from root cuttings in the winter — they will root and form new plants in a cold frame or greenhouse. It also sows itself quite freely.

The primulas in the Candelabra Section have their flowers arranged in whorls up the stems. The main flowering period is June and July. They are magnificent plants for growing with hostas and given moist conditions and partial shade they will quickly become naturalised. Among my favourites is P. japonica which is easy to grow and no doubt the best-known plant in this Section.

One of the best white-edged hostas is *H. crispula*. It has pale lilac flowers.

The colour is purplish red and it grows to about 45cm in height. There are some good named forms of this species, such as 'Miller's Crimson' (crimson, as the name suggests), and 'Postford White' which is white with a pink eye.

Primula aurantiaca is slightly shorter at 30cm when in flower. In July it produces bright reddish-orange flowers which look well with greyish or bluish hostas. The flowers of *P. beesiana* are bright rose-purple with a yellow centre and are carried on 60cm high stems. *P. bulleyana* is deep orange shaded with lighter orange and attains the same height. Also of the same height is *P. chungensis* whose flowers are pale orange with a red tube. *P. cockburniana* is orange-red and attains 30cm in height. A really striking species is *P. helodoxa*: the golden yellow flowers are carried on stems up to 1m in height. *P. pulverulenta* is claret red with a deeper centre and the 60cm tall stems are covered with a white 'meal' Bartley Strain is well-known and has pale pink flowers. The 'Asthore Hybrids' originated from several of the above species and they come in a range of colours for instance, orange, yellow

Among the earliest primulas to flower is *P. denticulata* and it will quickly make large clumps in a moist shady spot.

The best-known species of blue poppy is *Meconopsis betonicifolia.*

Primula vialii likes a cool, moist peaty soil.

dae is one of my favourites in this Section as it has sulphur-yellow flowers in very large heads, and they are carried on stems up to 1m in height during June and July. This primula likes plenty of moisture and will grow in quite boggy conditions. *P. secundiflora* has reddish-purple flowers in early summer and it grows to 60cm in height. Then there is *P. sikkimensis* after which the Section is named. It has fragrant yellow flowers in late spring and early summer, carried on 60cm high stems.

My final choice of primula (although I could make a very much longer list as there are so many exciting plants from which to choose) is *P. vialii* which is most unusual in that it has spikes of flowers rather like miniature kniphofias. They are violet and scarlet – a striking combination. It flowers in June and July and will grow to about 45cm in height, provided it has a cool moist soil with plenty of peat added.

Natural companions for primulas are the magnificent blue poppies or meconopsis. But while most of the primulas can be grown in alkaline soils the meconopsis require acid soils, plus plenty of humus and adequate moisture. A sheltered position is necessary and woodland is ideal. These perennials like a cool soil and also a cool partially shady aspect.

The best-known species is *Meconopsis betonicifolia* which produces its blue poppy flowers on 1.2m high stems in early summer. *M. grandis* flowers at the same time and will grow up to 1.5m tall. There is an excellent form of this species with very large flowers named 'Branklyn'. Some authorities now consider it should be called *M. x sheldonii* 'Branklyn'. All of these meconopsis should be regularly divided in September to ensure they remain young and vigorous. Divide about

apricot, salmon-pink and purple. They grow to a height of about 1m. 'Red Hugh' is another hybrid which I can strongly recommend on account of its brilliant crimson flowers carried on 45cm high stems.

The Sikkimensis Section of the genus *Primula* has some attractive species suited to our purpose. The inflorescence consists of a number of long-stalked, pendulous, bell-shaped flowers. *P. florin-*

every three years. Meconopsis are also easily raised from seeds which should be sown immediately they are ripe. Do not cover the seeds as they are very fine, and germinate in a cold frame or cool greenhouse.

Another meconopsis which should be in every scheme of the type we are discussing is *M. cambrica*. This is a native of Britain and it grows to 45cm in height. In late spring it produces yellow or orange poppies which are well set off by the attractive ferny foliage. It sows itself very freely and will quickly become naturalised in a woodland or mock-woodland scheme.

I would not be without *Polygonatum multiflorum* in this scheme for this British native produces, in the spring, white and green bells on 60cm high arching stems. It needs cool, moist, humus-rich soil and shady conditions when it will spread fairly quickly to form pleasing colonies. The foliage is attractive but may be attacked by sawflies in the summer.

The white bottle-brush-like flowers of *Cimicifuga racemosa* are most pleasing in the summer and they are carried on 1.5m high stems. It has attractive divided green foliage. And finally I can recommend *Astrantia major* for our scheme. In the summer and autumn it bears heads of greenish-white flowers with a green collar of bracts. It attains a height of 60cm when in flower.

Shade with dry soil

There is no doubt that if you have very dry soil in a shady spot, such as under a very large tree with a dense canopy of foliage, then yo are rather restricted in the choic of plants which will grow in suc conditions. The choice is no particularly exciting, as it is wit moist shade. Nevertheless on can manage to cover the soil wit plants and, I must be hones some of the plants are quit attractive. Most are of the groun cover type, and this is generall what is needed on such sites.

Firstly a few words on so preparation prior to planting. Di as deeply as you can, tree root permitting, and incorporat plenty of organic matter whic will help to conserve moisture Also it will be necessary to carr out regular watering — and heav watering — in dry weather t compensate for the great amoun of moisture taken out of the soil b the roots of the trees. A perman ent mulch of organic matter wi help to prevent the surface of th soil from drying out rapidly in ho weather. Regular topdressings c fertilisers in the spring will b necessary plus an application prior to planting.

I have an extremely difficul corner in my garden. The corne is formed by beech hedges. In thi corner is a laburnum, and on th other side of the hedge in m neighbour's garden there is massive syringa. The mass o roots in this corner is quit incredible and all I can do is t tickle the surface of the soi Needless to say, for much of th year the soil is extremely dry. Ye I manage to grow such plants a lamiastrum, symphytum an lamium.

Lamiastrum luteum 'Variegatum is also known as *Galeobdolo luteum* 'Variegatum' and *Lamiun galeobdolon* 'Variegatum', and would not be surprised if th name is changed again by th time this book is published! Any way, having given the synonyms hope that readers will know th

For dry shade there are epimediums, which make good ground cover with their attractive foliage. This one is *E. x youngianum* 'Niveum'.

Pulmonaria saccharata and its cultivars are excellent for dry soil and shade. This is a cultivar named 'Pink Dawn'.

plant to which I am referring. It is an extremely tolerant low growing ground cover plant with evergreen silver-splashed leaves. In moister conditions it is rampant but the excess growth is easily forked out. In late spring and early summer it produces spikes of yellow flowers.

Lamium maculatum cultivars are also very adaptable and form pleasing ground cover in dry

Lamium maculatum cultivars form pleasing ground cover in dry shade.

shade. The species has leaves with a central white stripe and in the spring spikes of pinkish-purple flowers are produced. Good cultivars include the bright rose-pink 'Roseum' and the salmon 'Salmonea'.

Pulmonaria saccharata has attractive foliage, the leaves being green marbled with white. It flowers in the spring, the blooms being pink. Height is 30cm when in flower and the foliage forms quite good ground cover. There are several cultivars such as 'Mrs Moon' with rose-pink flowers and 'Pink Dawn' of similar colour.

Although rather a coarse-leafed plant, I quite like *Symphytum grandiflorum* on account of its cream bell-shaped flowers which open from red-tipped buds. It flowers through the spring and well into the summer, attaining 20cm in height and forming very dense ground cover. In moist soils it spreads vigorously but it can be forked out if it exceeds its allotted space. But make sure you remove all the roots otherwise pieces left in the ground are likely to produce new plants. One of the

methods of propagation is from root cuttings.

Saxifraga x urbium can be grown virtually anywhere and it makes good dense ground cover with its evergreen foliage. Its leathery leaves are formed in rosettes and from the centre of these arise sprays of dainty pink flowers in May and June, on stems no more than 30cm in height. There is a form with yellow-spotted leaves called 'Aurea Punctata' but I find that the markings are more pronounced when the plant is grown in the sun.

Most people would consider that the epimediums rank among the most attractive plants suited to dry shady conditions. The foliage is attractive and makes good ground cover and in some it is prettily tinted in the spring. It is best trimmed off in the winter before new growth commences in the spring. The dainty flowers are carried on wiry stems in the spring. Although the plants tolerate dry conditions, better growth will be achieved if you supply them with adequate water during very dry periods. Epimediums spread quite vigorously by means of underground stems and the plants are best divided every three years or so immediately after flowering, when they are growing vigorously. There are many species and forms but the ones described here are among the best known and most easily available. *E. x youngianum* 'Niveum' is a white-flowered form with bronze foliage and it grows 15cm tall. *E. grandiflorum* 'Rose Queen' has bright pink flowers on 30cm high stems and pleasing green foliage of the same height.

Flowering later than most other epimediums, in June, *E. pinnatum* has bright yellow flowers on 22cm high stems. There is a number of forms with flowers in various shades of yellow and brownish orange.

9. Plants for hot and dry places

We progress from one extreme to another – from shady spots to very hot and dry situations. The latter can be difficult unless you choose the most suitable plants; for instance, some of those from the Mediterranean and similar areas — plants which are used to hot sun and maybe poor dry soils.

Similar conditions can exist in our gardens, at least during the summer. For example, you may have a bank in full sun which has a light, poor, dry soil. Or it may be a sheltered corner which acts as a sun trap in the summer.

You can in fact have a most pleasing planting scheme in such

A bank in full sun which has a light, poor, dry soil, is an ideal situation for a number of plants from the Mediterranean and similar areas. Many have silvery, woolly, glaucous or succulent leaves.

an arid situation. Many of the plants suited to these conditions have silvery or woolly foliage, or maybe glaucous foliage. Others may be succulent, such as the sedums. Some of the perennials with purplish foliage are also suited to hot situations.

To my mind one should try to emulate the arid conditions from which some of these plants originate. One way of doing this is to cover the soil between the plants with shingle or stone chippings, to give the impression of stony or rough rocky terrain. Benefits to be derived from this are moisture retention in the soil and control of germinating annual weed seeds.

Although I advocate choosing plants which thrive in hot dry conditions, it is best to encourage growth as much as possible by thoroughly preparing the soil before planting. Very poor dry conditions can result in stunted growth which, in a garden situation, does not look very pleasing, although it is a different matter in the wild.

So I would recommend digging the planting site as deeply as possible, ideally double digging or to two depths of the spade or fork. To each trench add a good quantity of organic matter such as well-rotted farmyard manure, garden compost, peat, leaf-mould or spent hops. This will help to conserve moisture during dry periods and this in turn should ensure better growth. Before planting it would be advisable to fork a general-purpose fertiliser into the top few centimetres of soil, especially if the soil is very poor. Thereafter annual top-dressings of fertiliser will be appreciated by the plants. Apply in the spring just as growth is commencing.

If you do not wish to cover the soil with shingle or stone chippings, then it would be a good idea to

Zauschneria californica is a native of the south and west United States and certainly needs full sun and very good drainage.

apply a mulch of organic matter to prevent the soil from drying out rapidly. See mulching in Chapter Fourteen. During the spring and summer try to carry out regular watering in dry weather. All of this will help to ensure better growth from your plants.

I have selected a range of interesting and colourful plants which are suited to hot dry situations, so let us now look at these in detail.

Zauschneria californica is a native of the south and west United States and it certainly needs full sun and very good drainage. It is best grown only in the warmer parts of the country as it may succumb to very cold winters.

This plant is attractive on account of its trumpet-shaped scarlet flowers which are carried in sprays during the summer and autumn. It somewhat resembles some of the species of fuchsia and is, in fact, commonly known as the Californian fuchsia. There is another attractive species named *Z. cana* which has very slender silver-grey leaves which contrast beautifully with the scarlet trumpet-shaped flowers.

From Italy comes *Anthemis cupaniana* which forms silver carpets of growth about 30cm in height. In fact, it makes very good ground cover, although it may die back in the winter. I find it is best to lift and divide this plant regularly in the spring, especially if it has died back and become straggly in the winter. This plant flowers in the summer and it literally smothers itself with pure white daisy flowers with yellow centres. I grow it in really poor dry conditions and it romps away and flowers profusely. It is an easy plant to propagate from cuttings of young growths — they can simply be stuck in the ground and will rapidly take root.

Centranthus ruber comes from various parts of Europe and grows to about 60cm in height. It has fleshy leaves which are greyish-green in colour and bears deep pink flowers very freely in the summer. To prove how lean a diet it can tolerate, I have seen it thriving in old walls where there is, of course, no soil at all. It particularly likes limy or chalky conditions. There is a white-flowered form called *C. r.* 'Albus' and also a very good deep red one named *C. r.* 'Atrococcineus'.

Phlomis viscosa is found in the wild in Syria and it has whorls of yellow flowers in June and July carried on stems up to 1m in height. The large heart-shaped leaves are rather rough in texture. The seed heads are attractive and should be left on the plant until they become tatty, which will be well into the winter. I consider them particularly useful for flower arranging as they can be dried for winter use.

The potentilla hybrids will provide bright splashes of colour in the summer with their flowers which resemble those of strawberries in shape. I find that they flower better in drier or poorer soils than in rich fertile conditions; and full sun is essential. There are many excellent hybrids from which to choose, such as 'Gibson's Scarlet' with bright scarlet blooms on stems up to about 45cm in height; 'Monsieur Rouillard' with 5cm wide double flowers in velvety

Centranthus ruber has fleshy leaves and flowers freely in summer. It can tolerate an extremely lean diet and will even grow in old walls.

crimson, of the same height; 'Wm. Rollisson' with semi-double blooms in brilliant orange, 45cm in height; and 'Yellow Queen' with deep yellow flowers and silvery foliage, of the same height. The flowering period is long — from June to August — and will be all the better if the plants are grown in lean soil conditions. These hybrids are completely trouble free plants and are long lived.

Phygelius capensis is a native of South Africa. It is rather shrubby in habit but it can be treated like a herbaceous plant and have the stems cut down in the autumn or winter. The flowering period extends from July until well into the autumn — in fact, flowering only stops when the frosts commence. The tubular flowers are bright red with a yellow throat and are carried on stems up to 1m in height. There is a form called *P. c.* 'Coccineus' which is reputedly brighter in colour and it has more yellow in the throat. I should mention that phygelius can be grown against a wall, when the plants will grow much taller — up to 2m in height — and will assume a shrubby habit of growth.

A charming thistle-like plant from Nepal is *Morina longifolia*. It forms rosettes of green thistle-like prickly leaves and from these 1m high stems arise in the summer carrying whorls of tubular hooded flowers in white and rose. It does better in the milder counties and may suffer in a severe winter. I grow it reasonably well in dry conditions, although I must admit that it makes better growth in a moist, but well-drained, soil.

Finally a few sedums with succulent leaves which revel in hot dry conditions, including very poor or stony soils. From the Far East comes *Sedum aizoon* with yellow flowers in the summer on stems up to 45cm in height. The flowers are tiny and are carried in flat heads. Even better in my opinion is *S. a.* 'Aurantiacum' which has deep yellow flowers carried on reddish stems. The blooms are followed by attractive red seed pods.

Sedum telephium 'Munstead Red' has dark green leaves which are flushed with purple. In late summer flat heads of flowers are carried on 45cm high stems and they are of an unusual colour — brownish red. They are rather sombre in appearance but nevertheless I find it an interesting plant for our purpose.

Phygelius capensis is a native of South Africa. The flowering period extends from July until well into the autumn.

Revelling in hot dry conditions, including very poor or stony soils, is the summer-flowering *Sedum aizoon,* a native of the Far East.

10. A grassy corner

If I were to omit grasses from this book I am sure I would have a shower of protests from readers — and rightly so, for the ornamental kinds are among the most exciting perennials available. What better subjects for contrasting with all kinds of plants, especially shrubs, and with architecture and paving. There are so many kinds to choose from — some have blue or grey foliage, others are variegated silver or gold, and many have impressive plumes of flowers.

Let us first look at the many possible uses in a garden of the ornamental grasses. As I have indicated, they are a good contrast for shrubs. For instance, I am particularly fond of planting *Phalaris arundinacea* 'Picta' around the base of purple-leafed shrubs, such as *Cotinus coggygria* 'Foliis Purpureis' or *Corylus maxima* 'Purpurea'. This grass has green and white striped leaves which contrast beautifully in colour and shape with the leaves of these shrubs. The bluish-grey foliage of *Helictotrichon sempervirens* also contrasts well with shrubs of this type.

Some grasses also make a good contrast for other hardy perennials. The white and green striped or glaucous grasses are, for instance, very useful for combining with herbaceous plants which have hot or strong colours, such as many of the cultivars of *Phlox paniculata*. There is no better foil for the brilliant reds and oranges of these border phloxes.

One of my favourite schemes is to plant a selection of grasses with yuccas and phormiums. All of the

The autumn-colouring *Liquidambar styraciflua* makes a magnificent background fo the giant plumes of *Cortaderia selloana.*

plants in this group should be widely spaced so that each clump shows to best advantage. For remember that all of these subjects make specimens of distinctive shape. The soil can then be covered with shingle or pebbles. I can assure readers that the result is superb. Such a group is best associated with modern architecture as it is, of course, rather formal in appearance. At Merrist Wood Agricultural College in Surrey there is a similar idea to this. Outside the modern dining hall there is a group of tall grasses, such as elymus and cortaderia, and the soil between them is covered with fairly large pebbles. The centrepiece of this group is an old hay spinner which has been painted black and this farm implement looks absolutely

Phormiums and ornamental grasses look most attractive together.

right among the grasses. Of course, not everyone can get hold of attractive old farm implements, but surely here is a position for a piece of sculpture — perhaps something contemporary.

Cortaderia is mainly used in private gardens as a centrepiece for the front lawn — a good if not very imaginative use. At Sheffield Park in Sussex cortaderia is planted at the edge of a lake, and it has a background of shrubs which are noted for their autumn tints. In the autumn the effect is stunning — the giant silvery-grey plumes of the cortaderia show up dramatically against the autumn foliage of the shrubs. Of course, this is garden design on a grand scale, but the idea could be copied even in a fairly small garden. Plant a cortaderia near a garden pool and plant a few autumn-colouring shrubs behind it.

There is no doubt that grasses of many kinds look good near water and, of course, they create beautiful reflections in the water. Choose those kinds which like a moist soil and combine them with such plants as gunnera, rheum, rodgersia and peltiphyllum, to provide a striking contrast in foliage shape.

At the Royal Horticultural Society's Garden at Wisley in Surrey there is a border of ornamental grasses of many kinds and they have been tastefully arranged according to height and colour. There is a wide expanse of lawn in front of this border to set them off. This scheme could be considered even in a fairly small garden — for instance, choose a sunny corner and have a small group of grasses of varying heights and colours. Such a group also looks attractive in the corner of a patio, for grasses and paving go very well together.

I have seen a pleasing way of

Miscanthus forms large tussocks to about 2 m in height, but does not get out of hand. The flowers are good for cutting and drying.

using grasses in various gardens — planting them in a raised bed with various other plants such as mahonias and yuccas. This makes an interesting feature in a paved area and, of course, the soil could be covered with shingle or pebbles to enhance the effect.

I hope that these ideas will appeal to readers, and I feel sure that many more ways of using grasses will come to mind when you consider a place for them in your own garden.

Just a few words on planting ornamental grasses. The best planting time is late spring as then they quickly become established. Autumn planting could mean some losses over the winter, particularly if your soil lies wet and cold. I should warn readers that cortaderia is particularly difficult to establish so do not be disappointed if you lose a plant or two, or if it takes a complete growing season for the plants to start making some growth. Corta-

deria is generally sold in containers nowadays to allow planting with minimum root disturbance. In fact, it is possible to buy a wide range of grasses in containers from good garden centres.

There is a vast range of ornamental grasses to choose from so I have selected about a dozen which should have wide appeal, and all of them should be easily obtained from a good garden centre or nursery.

Let us first consider the most popular grass of all — *Cortaderia selloana*. This is a stately plant which forms large clumps, and it is popular for lawn planting, but do consider other uses as outlined earlier in this chapter. It has long arching leaves and large silvery-grey plumes of flowers in late summer and autumn. When in flower it will reach a height of at least 2m. There is a form called 'Pumila' which is more compact in habit and one called 'Rendatleri' with silvery-pink plumes. 'Sunningdale Silver' has creamy-white plumes and attains about 2m in height. *C. fulvida* forms great clumps of leaves and has buff coloured flowers which appear in late June, much earlier than those of *C. selloana*. It is on the tender side and can only be recommended for mild areas. Even then the crown should be protected in the winter. Like all the grasses mentioned here, the plants are best grown in a sunny situation and in a well-drained soil. *Miscanthus sinensis* 'Zebrinus' forms large tussocks up to about 2m in height and has narrow green leaves with golden-yellow bars across the blades. This grass has many uses; for example, as a specimen clump in a lawn or shrub border, or in a group of grasses. It is especially good as a background for the border phloxes. In October pinky-brown silky flower heads are produced which are ideal for cutting and drying. Although a strong grower it is not rampant and will not, therefore, become a nuisance in the garden. This grass is suited to either moist or dry soils and therefore would also make a good waterside plant.

A dwarf tufted grass ideal for a frontal position in a bed or border is *Festuca glauca* with very narrow leaves which are greyish-blue in colour. It grows to about 20cm in height. Grow it in a bold group or drift for the best effect and give it a well-drained soil.

Another dwarf grass is *Molinia caerulea* 'Variegata' which again forms dense tufts. This grass, however, has green leaves which have an attractive cream margin. In October it produces purple-tinted panicles of flowers on stems up to 60cm in height. It is fairly slow to increase and therefore is best planted in fairly bold groups or drifts. It is not unduly fussy about soil provided drainage is adequate. I have occasion-

Molinia caerulea 'Variegata' is a dwarf, densely tufted grass with cream margins to the leaves. Purple-tinted flowers appear in October.

Although quite a rampant grower, *Phalaris arundinacea* 'Picta' is fairly easily dug up if it outgrows its allotted space.

74

ally planted this grass around the base of purple-leafed shrubs, in which situation it looks most pleasing.

Another grass which makes an interesting contrast to purple-leafed shrubs is *Phalaris arundinacea* 'Picta'. This is a taller kind, at about 60cm in height, and is quite a rampant grower, especially in moist fertile soils. In drier, poorer soils its rate of spread is slowed down. If it outgrows its allotted space it is fairly easily dug up with a garden fork, but make sure you remove all the rhizomes otherwise it will make new growth from them. This grass has green and white striped leaves, more white than green, so it appears as a very light-coloured plant. I like the dead foliage in the autumn and winter as it turns a very pale straw colour which contrasts well with any evergreen shrubs which may be close by. Towards the end of the winter this foliage becomes rather tatty, of course, at which stage it should be cut down to ground level.

Helictotrichon sempervirens forms dense clumps of foliage to about 60cm in height. It has very narrow leaves and they are a very bright blue-grey. A very useful grass for sunny spots, especially in association with purple-leafed shrubs or herbaceous plants. It does not spread and therefore is not a nuisance in any situation. In the summer it produces large attractive panicles of flowers which are carried on grey stems.

Also with blue-grey leaves, although much broader, is *Elymus arenarius*. The leaves attain a length of about 60cm and above these in the summer are borne spikes of blue-grey flowers. There is one drawback to this grass — it has a fantastically rapid spread and will quickly colonise large areas. But if you have a sizeable piece of ground which you want quickly covered with an effective

A dwarf tufted grass, ideal for a frontal position in a bed or border, is *Festuca glauca*. A bold group creates the best effect.

A useful grass for sunny spots, especially in association with purple-leafed shrubs or herbaceous plants, is *Helictotrichon sempervirens*.

ground cover plant, then here is the plant for you. It is an ideal choice for very poor soils and is also good for stabilising loose sandy soils, as may be found in some coastal gardens or on steep banks. Elymus is, incidentally, found growing naturally in coastal areas, especially on sand dunes. There is no denying the beauty of this grass with its fine bluish foliage, and it is such a pity that it cannot be recommended for small gardens.

To my mind one of the most beautiful grasses is *Milium effusum* 'Aureum', a form of a British native grass. It is at its best in the spring when it produces bright golden leaves. In the summer flowers of the same colour are produced. It is a dwarf grass, attaining no more than 60cm in height. It will sow itself, but not excessively, and is best planted in partial shade. A superb effect is achieved if it is planted with a blue spring-flowering plant, such as *Pulmonaria angustifolia*.

A form of the giant reed, *Arundo donax* 'Variegata' has leaves which are variegated cream and green. It will grow to 2m in height but unfortunately is rather tender and will only succeed in mild areas such as parts of Cornwall. Even in parts of the mild south-east it does not always prove very hardy. Its requirements are full sun and a sheltered position, although it will succeed in moist or dry soils. *Arundo donax* itself is hardier, thriving in the south and south-east, and the foliage is equally attractive, being bluish grey.

Glyceria maxima 'Variegata' is best grown as a waterside plant and it will reach a height of 1.2m when in flower. The 60cm long leaves are striped with pale yellow and are tinted with pink in the spring. In the summer greenish flowers are produced. Ideally this grass should be given a moist or

wet situation but in these conditions it will spread fairly rapidly. Growth will be more restrained in dry soils. It looks superb planted with other pool-side plants such as bog primulas and astilbes.

Growing to 2m in height, *Stipa gigantea* forms really dense clumps of growth. The flowers are most attractive in the summer as they are golden and each one terminates in a long awn. The flowers are carried in large heads. It is an adaptable grass, thriving in

dryish or moist soils.

Finally a word to flower arranger — remember that many of th grasses produce attractive flowe heads which can be cut and drie before they set their seeds, an these heads are ideal for using i winter arrangements. An arrange ment of different grasses on thei own can make an effectiv feature, especially in a corne which may have insufficient ligh for the well-being of pot plants.

Glyceria maxima 'Variegata' is best grown as a waterside plant and it will reach a height of 1.2 m when in flower.

11. Hiding the soil

A modern trend in gardening is to hide the soil as much as possible and an attractive way of accomplishing this is to plant ground cover plants. It is difficult to define the meaning of this term, for any plant which makes sufficiently dense growth to hide the soil could be called a ground cover plant. But generally speaking it implies the use of low-growing plants, generally below 1m in height. Suitable plants are those which form dense mats, carpets, hummocks or cushions of growth. Plants ideally should be evergreen so that they clothe the soil the year round, but a number of herbaceous plants are often used for ground cover. Plants which are to be used for ground cover are planted fairly close together so that within about twelve months they completely close up and hide the soil.

But why should we want to completely hide the soil? There are various reasons, one being aesthetic. Some soils are not very pleasing to look at, especially chalky types which often appear whitish or greyish when the surface dries out. Plants rarely look good against such a light-coloured background. Gravelly soils do not look very pleasing either — they appear rather poor and give the impression of dry barren land. The same applies to light sandy types. Clay soils are usually unattractive when they start to dry out in the spring and summer — often cracks appear in the surface. To my mind a covering of low-growing plants is far more appealing.

Another good reason for cover-

Some of the geraniums make dense ground cover and they are particularly suitable for dry conditions and do not mind shade.

ing the soil is to reduce weeding and soil cultivations. Low-growing plants can be mass planted between shrubs, trees and other taller plants, so making beds and borders much easier to maintain. If growth is sufficiently dense, ground cover plants will effectively suppress annual weeds — but not perennial weeds.

Ground cover plants are very useful for any area which is difficult to maintain, such as a steep bank. They can also be used for areas which you do not wish to spend much time maintaining — many people with large gardens often find it convenient

to use ground cover in various parts of the garden. It is far more labour saving than putting areas down to grass, which needs mowing at least once a week in the spring and summer. Besides, ground cover plants are far more interesting than grass — they create a better and different kind of texture. Grassing down large areas is not really very imaginative: it is simply an easy way out — at first.

In some situations ground cover plants are used to stabilize the soil: the roots permeate or ramify the soil and bind it together. Soil on a steep bank often needs stabilizing otherwise it would be eroded by heavy rain. The soil would be washed down to the bottom, leaving most of the bank devoid of topsoil. Soil in many seaside gardens also needs a dense growth of plants to prevent erosion. This applies to the very light, sandy, humus-deficient soils which are often characteristic of coastal gardens.

A final reason for ground cover — it is the most natural thing in the world to completely cover the soil! How often does one see bare soil in the wild in this country? Very rarely, unless there is something seriously wrong. Soil very quickly becomes covered with plants if, for some reason, it has become exposed. Of course, in a very dense woodland there may

well be insufficient light for plant growth beneath the canopy, but even in this situation one sometimes finds some plants which have adapted to these conditions. So why not copy nature and cover your soil?

Before planting ground cover plants, however, you must make sure that the soil is completely free of perennial weeds as these will not be suppressed but will simply grow up through the plants and will be impossible to remove.

It also pays to dig the soil deeply if possible and to add manure or garden compost, for the plants will be (or should be) left undisturbed for many years. Just before planting apply a general purpose fertiliser to the soil

surface and lightly prick it in.

The next thing to consider is the number of plants per square metre of soil surface in order to achieve complete cover within about twelve months. For small growing plants, such as ajuga, asperula, prunella and luzula, one could plant eight to ten per square metre. For larger plants like geranium, bergenia, polygonum and hosta, five per square metre would be sufficient.

Until the plants grow together you will need to weed between them. Annual weeds can either be pulled out by hand or they could be hoed off, maybe using an onion hoe. Alternatively one could use the herbicide propachlor to kill germinating weed seeds — see Weeding in Chapter Fourteen.

An unusual idea for ground cover in woodland conditions is to mass plant hardy cyclamen. They have attractive foliage which forms very dense carpets.

The ajugas, with their mat-forming habit of growth, are ideal for ground cover between shrubs. Here is an attractive combination of ajuga and purple berberis.

Now let us consider some suitable perennials for use as ground cover. I will be describing both evergreen perennials for all-the-year-round cover and also herbaceous kinds which die down in the autumn.

The ajugas, with their mat-forming habit of growth, are ideal for ground cover between shrubs, beneath deciduous shrubs or beneath trees. They will grow in most kinds of soil but they do appreciate moist conditions, in which they make the best growth. They will take sun or shade but are most at home in semi-shaded conditions. They do not like very hot dry situations. Most of the ajugas spread fairly rapidly but this is not much of a problem for as soon as they outgrow their allotted space they are easily checked by forking out the growth. They are evergreen, although some become rather sparse in the winter.

The most popular kinds of ajuga are the cultivars of the native *A. reptans*. This plant is commonly found in the countryside, particularly beside streams and in moist meadows, where it produces its blue flowers in May and June. But the cultivars are more attractive as far as foliage is concerned as most are variegated. For instance, there is 'Variegata' which has grey-green leaves variegated with cream. This is probably the most popular cultivar grown. I am very fond of 'Atropurpurea' which has dark bronze-purple leaves and makes a pleasant contrast with silver-leafed plants such as *Stachys lanata*. 'Rainbow' (also known as 'Multicolor') has green and bronze leaves which are mottled with yellow and they also have a pink flush — a very striking colour combination. Another exciting colour combination is to be found in 'Burgundy Glow'. It has the same leaf colour as 'Variegata' but the leaves are also heavily flushed with reddish purple. All of these cultivars have spikes of blue flowers, but there is a white-flowered one called 'Alba', with plain green foliage.

Asperula odorata (also known as *Galium odoratum*) is a superb little carpeting plant which, however, dies down in the winter. It is a British native plant and it has bright, fresh green, whorled leaves which are an attraction in themselves. In the spring it is spangled with tiny white flowers. There is no better carpeting plant for a woodland setting — this is its natural habitat. But it is also suitable as ground cover between shrubs. It likes a cool moist soil and dappled shade. Although it grows quite vigorously in the right conditions it by no means becomes a nuisance and is easily kept in check.

Some of the geraniums make very dense ground cover but their foliage dies down in the autumn. They are particularly suitable for dry conditions and do not mind shade, so they are ideal for growing under trees, for example. They also look good in a woodland garden. On the other hand they will thrive in moist soils and full sun, so they are very adaptable. They can be thoroughly recommended for planting between shrubs in a bed or border. One of my favourites is *Geranium macrorrhizum* 'Album'. It has very aromatic foliage, the scent of which is much liked by some people, including myself, but disliked by others. But it is only apparent when you pinch it or brush it with your hands. This geranium has an exceptionally long flowering period: it starts in late spring or early summer and goes on until late summer or early autumn. As the name suggests, the blooms are white. Other geraniums, such as *G. endressii* mentioned in Chapter Two, are also very suitable for ground cover among shrubs or beneath trees.

Among the evergreen perennials suitable for ground cover are the bergenias with their large, rounded, leathery, shiny foliage. This foliage makes quite a dense covering and effectively suppresses annual weed growth. The bergenias flower in the spring and produce short spikes of blooms. Unfortunately in the winter the leaves can become rather shabby, but in the spring the old ones can be removed as the new foliage is being produced. They are tremendously adaptable plants, thriving in sun or shade and any type of soil, moist or dryish. However, I find that they make better growth in moist soils and they do not seem particularly keen on my very chalky soil. There are some good species to choose from, and in recent years a range of superb hybrids has been produced.

B. cordifolia is a very popular species with deep green leaves which make an excellent background for the magenta flowers. *B. crassifolia* has thick leaves and

The evergreen bergenias make good ground cover in sun or shade and any type of soil. *B. cordifolia,* shown here, is a popular species.

there are pink and red-flowered forms available. *B. x schmidtii* has bright rich green foliage which is toothed at the edges. It may come into flower as early as February and the blooms are clear pink. This is a hybrid plant, the result of a cross between *B. ciliata ligulata* and *B. crassifolia.* As I said above, there are some excellent modern hybrids to choose from such as 'Ballawley' with crimson flowers borne on red stems. The shiny green leaves are less evergreen than those of most other bergenias. It should be given a sheltered position, free from cold winds, and ideally a good fertile soil. Then there is 'Abendglut' or

'Evening Glow' with crimson-purple flowers. Although there are many more I could list, I must certainly not leave out 'Silberlicht' or 'Silver Light' with pure white flowers which become pinkish as they age.

In the winter the leaves of most bergenias turn purplish or have a reddish tinge. This is a particular feature of *B. cordifolia* 'Purpurea' whose leaves become quite purplish in the winter. It has vivid magenta flowers on red stems.

The bergenias have many uses as ground cover: for instance, they look superb planted around the base of spring-flowering Japanese cherries, and they are the obvious choice for shrub beds

Cultivars of *Polygonum affine* will form dense mats given an open position in full sun and a reasonably moist soil.

Prunella grandiflora cultivars are not used much for ground cover. Yet they are easy to grow and, as can be seen, form dense carpets.

and borders, especially when associated with spring-flowering shrubs. Their foliage is often used as a contrast with sword-like leaves and with paving — the plants help to soften the edges of paths and patios.

Some of the polygonums make fairly dense mats of growth and are therefore ideal for ground cover, particularly in the more open positions. They do like adequate sun and they will grow in virtually any type of soil, provided there is a reasonable amount of moisture at all times. Cultivars of *Polygonum affine* are among the best for our purpose, like 'Darjeeling Red' with crimson flower spikes from early to late summer or autumn. 'Donald Lowndes' has larger spikes of rose-coloured flowers and again has this long flowering period. The flowers deepen in colour as the summer advances. In the species itself the flowers are pink. This species and its cultivars spread quite vigorously but the plants are easy to keep in check — just chop out excess growth with a spade. Then there is *P. vacciniifolium* with spikes of rose-pink flowers during summer and autumn. It literally covers itself with blooms so that it appears a solid carpet of pink. This one certainly needs good drainage and full sun for best results, but given these conditions is an easily grown plant. I rather like planting the polygonums at the front of a shrub border or bed so that they partly spread over the path and help to soften the harsh edges.

The cultivars of *Prunella grandiflora* do not seem to be used to any great extent as ground cover — at least I have not seen them used very much for this purpose. Yet they make good cover at the front of shrub beds or borders with their very low mats of growth. They are easily grown plants and will take virtually any soil, but will not make very good growth if the situation is very hot and dry. The plants have dark green toothed leaves and produce their flowers in short spikes during the summer and early autumn. They spread fairly quickly if conditions are to their liking but they are no trouble to keep in check. Cultivars one should grow are 'Loveliness' with lilac flowers; 'Pink Loveliness' with pink blooms; and 'White Loveliness' with white flowers, of course. For best results the prunellas should be lifted and divided every three or four years to keep them young and vigorous. They retain their leaves in the winter.

Another plant that does not seem to be used to any great extent for ground cover is *Luzula sylvatica*, yet I have used it very effectively for this purpose. It produces dense tufts of deep, shiny green, grass-like foliage and panicles of brown flowers in the summer.

What is more, the plant is ever-green. There is a form with narrow cream margins to the leaves called 'Marginata'. These are ideal plants for shady conditions such as a woodland garden, under trees or between shrubs. Any type of soil is suitable, but better growth is made in moist conditions; fairly dry soils are tolerated.

I have by no means exhausted the range of suitable ground cover perennials — in fact, I have only recommended some of my favourites. There are many other plants equally suitable and some are included in other chapters. Perhaps it would be as well to list these, to give you a wider choice of plants. You will find descriptions of them in the appropriate chapters and any particular cultural needs.

Luzula sylvatica is an evergreen tufted grass-like plant suited to ground cover in shade, such as between shrubs or in a woodland garden.

12. Pots and patios

A trend in gardening today is to grow plants in pots, tubs, urns, troughs and other kinds of garden containers on patios, terraces and other paved areas. This is far from a new idea, for the ancient Greeks and Romans, and other civilisations, were growing trees and other plants in containers a couple of thousand years ago. The main reason it has become popular again is because gardens of modern houses are generally very small and it is a good way to utilise available space for growing plants. Apart from this, a patio or terrace is much enhanced by plants in containers and can even be given a sub-tropical atmosphere if appropriate plants are chosen.

Although there is much written on suitable plants for containers, authors, for some reason, seem to neglect the use of perennial plants. Instead they seem to concentrate on spring and summer bedding plants, shrubs, trees, conifers and fruits. Yet there are several perennials which are admirably suited to this method of cultivation: so let us consider some of them, and also suitable types of container for them, as the containers should complement the plants grown in them.

My favourite plants for containers are the South African agapanthus which flower in the summer. They have handsome strap-shaped foliage and lily-like flowers, mainly in shades of blue, but also white. *A. campanulatus* is an attractive species with sky-blue flowers, and there is a white form called 'Albus'. The 'Headbourne Hybrids' have flowers

Any of the hostas can be grown in containers and they give a luxuriant foliage effect on a patio, terrace or in a courtyard.

varying from pale blue to deep violet-blue. *A. orientalis* is a good shade of blue but it will need frost protection in the winter. The container could be moved under cover. There is a white form, 'Albus'. I think the agapanthus look superb in terracotta pots or urns as this brick colour contrasts beautifully with the blue or white flowers. These plants are also well set off in wooden tubs or half barrels. Both of these containers would, incidentally, be admirably suited to cottage gardens, as they have a

somewhat informal appearance. Hemerocallis have similar foliage to the agapanthus and they produce a long succession of lily-like flowers during the summer. They do like a moist soil so one will need to keep a regular eye on watering. There are many dozens of cultivars to choose from in a wide range of colours, so it would be better for readers to choose those which most appeal. I like to see hemerocallis in the same types of container as recommended for the agapanthus.

Some of the tall-growing

campanulas really look at home in wooden tubs or terracotta containers and this combination is an excellent choice for a cottage garden. I would recommend *C. lactiflora* with pale blue flowers on 1.2m high stems; *C.l.* 'Prichard's Variety' with violet-blue flowers and of the same height; *C. latifolia* 'Alba' with white flowers, 1.2m high; *C.l.* 'Brantwood' in violet-purple, 1.2m; *C. persicifolia* 'Snowdrift' in white, 1m; and *C. p.* 'Telham Beauty', deep blue, 1m. All flower over a long period in the summer. *Euphorbia wulfenii* makes a large plant up to 1.2m in height and it has attractive greyish foliage. In spring and summer it carries large heads of greenish-yellow flowers. It is probably best grown in a wooden tub or half barrel, at least 45cm in diameter and depth due to its size.

Any of the hostas can be grown in containers and they give a luxuriant foliage effect on a patio, terrace or in a courtyard. I have recommended a good selection in Chapter Eight so I will not repeat what has already been described. To my mind they look particularly good in some form of modern container, such as a concrete or asbestos tub or vase, placed in a modern setting. But this is just a personal choice and other people may prefer terracotta or wooden containers for them.

Phormiums give an exotic touch to a patio or terrace but they will need fairly large containers, such as wooden tubs or half barrels about 60cm in diameter by 60cm deep. I have recommended some phormiums in Chapter Six.

My final choice is rodgersia which I like to see in modern concrete containers in a contemporary setting. Like the phormiums, these are also grown for their foliage effect. Again readers should refer to Chapter Six for a selection of species.

So far I have said nothing about sun or shade, and this is, of course, very important — not all patios or terraces are sunny and very often courtyards are permanently shady. So below I have given an indication of suitable conditions for all the plants mentioned in this chapter.

Agapanthus — partial shade best, but will take full sun.

Campanula — will take full sun or partial shade.

Euphorbia — partial shade best, but will take full sun.

Hemerocallis — at home in the sun or in partial shade.

Hosta — best in shade but will take full sun.

Phormium — full sun is necessary.

Rodgersia — shade is best but will take sun.

Hemerocallis hybrids produce a long succession of flowers during the summer and therefore are well worth planting in a container.

Planting and aftercare

The choice of containers is, of course, up to individual readers and one will find a very big range to choose from at a good garden centre. I have given an indication of the types available but they come in a wide range of shapes and sizes, some modern, others traditional. I feel, though, I should say a little more about size of containers for perennials, although in one or two instances I have given this. The minimum size for healthy growth would be 45cm in diameter by 45cm deep. Some of the larger perennials, like phormiums, would need a container about 60cm by 60cm. Most subjects would need to be planted singly to allow them room to grow but for the smaller subjects, like some of the hostas, for instance, one would be able to plant

Agapanthus, like these 'Headbourne Hybrids', look superb in terracotta pots as this brick colour contrasts beautifully with the blue lily-like flowers. These perennials flower for a long period in the summer.

perhaps two or three plants in each container.

All garden containers should have drainage holes in the base, but if you find that half barrels or wooden tubs do not, then you will have to drill some drainage holes, ideally about 2.5cm in diameter. Before planting, the drainage holes will need covering with a layer of crocks (broken clay flower pots), stones or pieces of brick to prevent soil from blocking them and to make sure excess water is able to drain away. A layer about 5cm deep is generally sufficient. Over this drainage material place a layer of roughage, such as coarse peat, leaf-mould or broken turves, to prevent soil washing down into the drainage material and blocking it. A layer about 2.5cm deep will be adequate. Now you can fill up with compost, to within 2.5cm of the top of the container to allow space for watering. Firm it moderately well with your hands.

A suitable compost is John Innes potting compost No. 2 which is freely available in bags from garden centres. If you cannot obtain No. 2 then use No. 1, even though this has less fertiliser in it. The plants are planted in the normal way, making sure the roots are well spread out and not crammed into small holes. After planting water them in thoroughly — an indication of when sufficient water has been applied is when it starts to trickle out of the bottom of the container.

Of course, if you do not want to hump around heavy planted containers, they can be placed in their final positions before filling with compost.

Maintenance of plants in containers consists of regular watering — apply water whenever the surface of the compost starts to become dry. And each time apply sufficient to wet the compost right the way through — water should start to trickle out of the bottom of the container.

In the summer when plants are in full growth it is a good idea to give an occasional feed with liquid fertiliser, for the food supply in the compost is quickly depleted and some of it is leached out by the regular watering of the plants. Give a liquid feed about every two or three weeks during the growing period. In the spring each year the plants benefit from a topdressing of general purpose granular fertiliser, which should be lightly pricked into the surface. A very small handful to each container is adequate.

Take the usual precautions against slugs and snails in the spring (see Chapter Fourteen) for they even get into containers in search of food.

As soon as the plants seem to be outgrowing their containers they will need to be lifted, divided and replanted, otherwise the containers will become tightly packed with roots and then the plants will not make good growth — also it will be extremely difficult to remove the plants when eventually you do decide to lift and divide. It is difficult to say how often you will need to lift and divide, for it depends on the vigour of each type of plant, but in my experience it is necessary every two or three years. Before replanting divisions you will need to prepare the containers again as outlined earlier on, using fresh compost. Details of division will be found in Chapter Fourteen.

In the autumn any dead stems and foliage should be removed to maintain a neat and tidy appearance. In fact, the beauty of growing herbaceous plants in containers is that when they have lost their interest in the autumn the containers can be moved off the patio, etc., and hidden in some other part of the garden.

Then as the plants are coming into flower or leaf in the following year they can be moved back on to the patio. For the spring, when many herbaceous plants are only just coming into growth, you could have containers of spring bedding plants and bulbs. When these are over the containers could be moved elsewhere and the perennials put back into place.

Of course, it is not easy to move planted containers due to their weight and the larger ones are virtually impossible to move by lifting and carrying. If you intend to move containers as suggested above then you will need to provide yourself with suitable equipment for the purpose. You could, for instance, invest in a sack trolley. This would be useful for moving other heavy items around the house and garden and need not be used purely for containers. A sack trolley is a two-wheeled trolley with a flat platform near to the ground. It has long upright handles which are used to push it. To move a container with such a trolley, first tip the container and slide the platform of the trolley underneath. Then position the container against the back of the trolley. Now tip back the trolley and push. Instead of buying a sack trolley you could, perhaps, make a low flat trolley with castors. The platform need be only slightly larger than your largest container and can be made of timber. Castors can be purchased in many hardware stores and are simply screwed on underneath — one in each corner. To move a container with this, tip the container and slide the trolley underneath. Push the container to the centre and then pull along the trolley with a piece of rope.

13. Small town gardens

The gardens of modern town houses are very often extremely small and therefore the owners of these so-called pocket handkerchief gardens need to consider very carefully the kinds of plants that are to be grown. Plant size has to be scaled down if you are going to grow a reasonable range of plants. Fortunately there is a big range of shrubs and hardy perennials which are suited to very small beds or narrow borders.

I do not think, however, that every single plant in a tiny plot should be of dwarf or miniature stature — have one or two larger specimen shrubs or perennials to add variation. For instance, it may be possible to have a large rheum or cynara in a corner or by a patio.

But generally speaking you will need to go for small plants to fill the beds and borders. You should be careful about having straight borders in a very small garden for they can make the garden look even smaller. For instance, if you have a border down one side of the plot it could make the garden look quite narrow. So if you decide to go in for a conventional border then do consider very carefully where it would best be sited. The width of the border must be considered in relation to its length. Try to avoid having an extremely narrow border (say in the region of 60 cm) as it is then virtually impossible to arrange groups of plants effectively. A better width is 1 to 1.2m and if you could manage a length of 4 to 5m then it would be well proportioned.

Not every plant in a small garden should be dwarf. Here is a specimen of *Hydrangea sargentiana,* with dwarf astilbe and ground cover epimedium.

To my way of thinking (although I do not wish to influence the reader too much in this instance) an island bed or border might be a better proposition for a very small garden and this can, in fact, give the impression of more space — the exact opposite to a straight border down one side. The island bed could be placed in the lawn — not necessarily in the centre but perhaps towards one corner of the plot or towards one side (but not hard up against the boundary as this defeats the object). An island bed looks good in the lawn of an open-plan front garden, which most modern town houses seem to have these days.

Of course, in a small garden you would probably not wish to devote an island bed or a border to perennials. It would be far better to have mixed plantings of shrubs, perennials, bulbs, annuals and so on, to ensure some colour and interest at all times of the year.

A mixed planting scheme is probably best for small beds and borders, including hardy perennials, conifers, small shrubs, and half-hardy perennials.

The free-flowering *Oenothera* 'Fireworks' attains only 45 cm in height.

It would be best to try to site your beds or borders where they will receive a good deal of sun as then you will be able to grow a wider range of plants. But if part of the bed or border is shaded for all or part of the day then do remember that in this situation a collection of shade-loving plants could be grown. I have given a good selection in Chapter Eight. Many of these subjects are, as you will see, of dwarf stature; admirably suited to the small plot. Do not forget that one or two perennials could, perhaps, be grown in containers on a terrace or patio — see Chapter Twelve. These are a few ideas on the ways of using perennials in a small town garden. Let us now consider some small perennials which could be used in mixed beds and borders.

Small-growing perennials

There are several achilleas that could be used, including *A. clypeolata,* 45cm, which has yellow flowers from May to June and silver foliage. Provide full sun and good drainage for best results.

Some of the dwarf aquilegias would be well worth growing and they flower in May and June. I can recommend the following species: *A. alpina,* 45cm, blue flowers; *A. caerulea,* 30cm, white and light blue; *A. canadensis,* yellow with distinctive bright red spurs, 60cm; *A. glandulosa,* 30cm, blue and white; and 'Hensol Harebell', 45cm, rich deep blue, a superb hybrid.

For the autumn one should not forget the dwarf asters which are ideally suited to a small bed or border. They are vigorous spreaders and will possibly need lifting and dividing in the spring each year to keep them in check — and, of course, to ensure that they remain young and free flowering. I have given a list of dwarf cultivars in Chapter Two so there is no point in repeating it here. Dwarfs are those ranging from about 30 to 45cm in height. *Campanula carpatica* grows to only 15cm in height and blooms in the summer. There are various forms such as the violet-blue 'Isobel' and the white 'White Star'. *C. lactiflora* 'Pouffe' has lavender-blue flowers from July to September and grows to only 15cm.

Some of the smaller perennials mentioned in Chapter Two would be suitable for our purpose, and these include *Coreopsis verticillata* 'Grandiflora', erigerons, *Geranium endressii* cultivars, geums, *Helenium* 'Wyndley', pulmonaria, *Salvia superba* 'Lubeca', *Sedum spectabile* and stokesia. Dianthus are also very suitable, especially the border pinks like 'Dad's Favourite' in white with brown markings; 'Excelsior', deep rose-pink; the pale pink 'Inchmery' and the white, very fragrant 'Mrs Sinkins'.

Try some heucheras, which reach only about 45cm in height when in flower — which is for most of the summer. There is the famous mixed strain called 'Bressingham Hybrids', as well as named varieties like 'Red Spangles', crimson-scarlet, 'Scintillation', purplish red, and 'Sparkler', carmine and scarlet. Do not forget some of the small-growing hostas for their foliage effect, like *H. albomarginata, H. crispula, H. lancifolia* and *H. tardiflora*.

The liatris are very reliable perennials, flowering in the summer and growing happily in any well-drained soil provided they receive adequate sun. They are unusual plants in that the flower spikes open from the top downwards — most plants with spikes of flowers open them from the bottom upwards. *Liatris spicata* is the best known, with purplish flowers, but there is also *L. pycnostachya* with purplish-crimson spikes.

Linums flower mainly in early summer and I am particularly fond of *L. narbonense* which has flowers in a superb shade of blue. *L. perenne* has beautiful sky-blue flowers. Both plants reach only 45cm in height when in flower and are easily grown in a well-drained soil and sunny spot.

I have mentioned one or two oenotheras in the chapter which deals with scent. Most of those are rather too tall for our purpose but there are a few dwarfish kinds which would be suitable. For instance, there is 'Fireworks' with bright yellow flowers from red buds, height 45cm. *O. missouriensis* forms mats of growth and has huge pale yellow flowers. All of these plants flower over a long period in the summer. Provide good drainage and a reasonable amount of sun.

The potentilla hybrids will provide bright splashes of colour in beds and borders provided they are placed in a sunny position. They flower over a long period and therefore well deserve a place in the small garden. Some varieties have been given in Chapter Nine.

Serratulas are superb plants for the small garden yet it is suprising

Every inch of space is used in this small garden. A red centranthus has found a niche at the side of the steps.

Sisyrinchiums are dwarf members of the iris family and are easily grown in light well-drained soil and full sun.

Aster alpinus is an excellent choice for a small bed or border. It attains only about 15cm in height and is early flowering.

how rarely they are seen i private gardens. Maybe this i because people just do not know about them. They are like min ature centaureas and are easy t grow in any type of soil and sunny situation. *S. shawii* is th best-known species with mauve purple flowers on 30cm high branching stems. The flowerin period is autumn, which is usefu for there are not many sma plants which bloom at that time o the year.

Sisyrinchiums are members o the iris family and have grassy foliage. They are easy to grow in light well-drained soil in full sun There are quite a few species to choose from but I find the follow ing two as good as any: *S. angust ifolium* with pale violet flower from June to August, and *S brachypus* with golden-yellow flowers over the same period You should be able to obtain these plants from a nurseryman specialising in hardy perennials. The veronicas are of very easy culture provided drainage is good and they are planted in a sunny spot. They flower over long periods in the summer. Some are quite tall plants, so you will have to choose carefully. All of the fol lowing are of dwarf stature and ideally suited to tiny beds and borders. *V. gentianoides* grows to 60cm and has light blue flowers. The form 'Nana' reaches only 30cm in height. *V. incana* is a superb plant with its grey foliage and deep blue flowers. Height is 45cm. I like white veronicas also and can particularly recommend *V. spicata* 'Alba' at 45cm in height. Another *spicata* variety is 'Crater Lake Blue' with vivid ultramarine flowers and a height of 30cm. From July to Septem ber the hybrid 'Wendy' produces a succession of blue flowers which are well set off by the silvery-grey foliage. The height is about 45cm when in flower.

14. Cultural hints

To get the best from perennials it is necessary to treat them well and therefore I will round off the book with some useful basic cultural hints.

Soil preparation

Good soil preparation prior to planting perennials is vital for success as many of the plants will remain where they are planted for several years. If you are preparing a bed or border it is advisable to double dig the soil — that is, to two depths of the spade. This will help to ensure a deep root run and can help the drainage of excess water. It is best to add some form of organic matter to the soil as you dig, such as well-rotted farmyard manure, garden compost, peat, spent hops, leaf-mould or shredded bark. This should be placed in the bottom of each trench. On light sandy or chalky soils organic matter helps to conserve moisture during dry periods. On heavier soils such as clays it will help to improve drainage, as it has the effect of opening up such soils, in which case excess water is able to drain through to the lower layers. It is also a good idea to mix into the surface of heavy soils a good quantity of coarse sand or grit to further ensure adequate drainage.

During digging remove any perennial weeds, including the roots, as these are very difficult, if not impossible, to control once perennial plants are established. If there is much perennial weed on the site it would be best to let it lie fallow for several months and to treat the weeds with a herbicide such as glyphosate. Any annual weeds could be controlled with paraquat.

Ideally one should dig the site in the autumn so that the soil is exposed to the elements over the winter and also has a chance to settle. Planting can then take place in the spring, which is a suitable time for most plants.

About a week before planting a topdressing of a general purpose fertiliser can be given and this should be lightly pricked into the soil surface. Apply at the rate of 56–113g per 1sq m. Before planting, the roughly dug surface will need breaking down with a fork to create a reasonably fine tilth. It will also need to be firmed, which is best accomplished by systematically treading over the site with your heels.

Planting techniques

Most perennials can be planted in the spring, during March or April. Some people, however, prefer autumn planting, and this is acceptable provided the soil is very well drained, and is not prone to lying wet and cold over the winter. These conditions could result in the death of many young perennials. A hand trowel can be used for planting small clumps but for larger crowns a spade would be the more suitable tool. Take out a hole deep enough to allow the plants' roots to dangle down to their full length.

On no account cram the roots into a hole which is too small. The crown of the plant, where the buds are situated, should be at soil level after planting. Firm in the plants really well with your hands or heels, depending on the size of the clump.

These days many perennials are bought in containers (generally plastic bags) from garden centres and these can be planted at any time of the year provided the soil is not wet or frozen. They can even be planted when in full bloom. The way to plant these is to make a hole slightly larger than the soil ball of the plant, remove the plant from its container, stand it in the hole, replace the soil around the plant and firm well in. The idea is to disturb the roots as little as possible so that the plant becomes quickly established. So on no account remove the soil from around the roots. If the plant is in a plastic bag this container should be carefully cut away from the rootball with a knife.

Weeding

There are various methods of controlling weeds among perennials. There is hoeing, and this is effective provided it is carried out when the weeds are in the seedling stage and the surface of the soil is dry. Choose a warm breezy day so that the weeds quickly shrivel and die. Hoeing is hard work if you allow weeds to become large. Hand pulling can be carried out, first using a small border fork to loosen the soil.

You should only be troubled with annual weeds if soil preparation was thorough prior to planting. But if the odd perennial weed does appear it should be dug out with a border fork, taking care to remove all the roots. If a perennial weed grows up through the centre of a plant then the only way to remove it is to lift the plant, shake away all the soil from the roots and then try to pull out the weed. This should only be done in the autumn or early spring, and not when the plant is in full growth.

There is a herbicide which is safe to use among perennials to control annual weeds and it is based on the chemical propachlor. It is supplied in granular form and the granules should be sprinkled evenly over the soil according to the maker's instructions. The soil must be weed free and moist at the time of application. Afterwards do not disturb the soil surface in any way otherwise you will destroy the effect. This herbicide kills weeds just as the seeds are germinating and the effect can last for up to eight weeks, after which you will need to re-apply. It will not control established weeds.

Watering

For good growth and flowering, watering should be carried out in the spring and summer whenever the top 2.5cm of the soil surface starts to dry out. As indicated in the other chapters there are some perennials which will make poor growth if soil conditions become very dry. During dry periods or drought the aim should be to keep the top 15cm of soil moist at all times. This is best achieved by the use of a garden sprinkler attached to a hose, but check with your local water authority first in case a licence is needed. It is essential to keep newly planted perennials well supplied with moisture and remember that in the spring soil can dry out very rapidly.

Feeding

All perennials will benefit from an annual application of a general purpose fertiliser applied in April or May as a topdressing. Sprinkle it evenly over the soil surface between the plants, at a rate of 56–113g per 1sq m, and lightly fork it into the soil. If you intend using a mulch (see Mulching) the fertiliser should be applied first. It should also be applied prior to an application of herbicide (see Weeding).

Foliar feeding helps to boost growth in the summer but this should not be considered a substitute for topdressing in the spring. There are many foliar feeds on the market and they should be used according to the manufacturers' instructions.

Basically the liquid fertiliser is diluted with water and the solution applied to the foliage either with a sprayer or with a rose watering can.

Mulching

Mulching involves placing a layer of organic matter over the soil surface around and between the plants. This surface covering will suppress the growth of annual weeds so that weeding becomes unnecessary, and it helps to prevent the soil from drying out during periods of drought. Many perennials appreciate a mulch, especially those which need moist soil conditions.

A mulch should be applied to moist, weed free soil, after an application of fertiliser in the spring. It needs to be about 7.5cm deep if it is to prevent the growth of annual weeds. A mulch will not suppress the growth of any perennial weeds that may be in the beds or borders.

Suitable mulching materials include well-rotted farmyard manure, garden compost, peat, leaf-mould, spent hops, rotted lawn mowings and pulverised or shredded bark. The only materials which will supply some plant foods are manure, compost, leaf-mould, lawn mowings and bark. In my opinion the best mulching material for plants in a woodland setting is leaf-mould as this looks the most natural. Shredded bark also looks good in such a setting.

In beds and borders any of the above materials can be used, but to my mind the most pleasing appearance is provided by peat, leaf-mould or bark. Very light-coloured materials, like spent hops, do not give a very natural-looking appearance.

It is best to top up the mulch each spring if necessary but you will find that some materials, particularly bark, are very slow to decompose and it may be un-

necessary to apply fresh mulch each year. At the other extreme spent hops very quickly decompose.

Staking

Although the trend today is for self-supporting perennials which do not need staking or supporting many gardeners will have some plants which need a little help to keep them upright. Plants with thin floppy stems, such as *Aster acris,* are best supported with twiggy hazel sticks or pea sticks. These should be inserted around and between the plants just as the new shoots are being produced in the spring. The stems will then grow up through the sticks, eventually hiding them, and they will be well supported. Make sure the height of the sticks does not exceed the eventual height of the particular plant — in fact, they should be a little shorter so that the plant flowers above the supports.

Perennials which have a few tall heavy flower spikes, such as delphiniums, will need each stem tied in to a stout bamboo cane. The canes should be slightly shorter than the eventual height of the spikes, but should adequately support the often heavy spikes of flowers. Insert the canes before growth becomes over 1m in height, and regularly tie in the stems with raffia or soft garden string. It is best to insert the canes behind the stems so that they are hidden.

Pest and disease control

Slugs and snails are often a problem in the spring, eating the new shoots of many plants as they emerge through the soil. Perennials like delphiniums and lupinus are particularly susceptible to attack. Sprinkle methiocarb slug pellets around the plants just as growth is commencing. Alternatively use pellets based on metaldehyde, or use the cheaper slug bran or a liquid slug killer.

Aphids or greenfly can be easily controlled in the spring and summer by spraying the plants with one of the modern systemic insecticides which are taken in by the plants and therefore are not washed off the leaves by rain. They remain effective for many weeks. They will also control many other sucking and biting insects.

Asters and some other perennials are liable to be attacked by mildew which can seriously disfigure growth. It appears as a white powdery covering on the leaves and shoot tips. Immediately it is noticed spray with one of the modern systemic fungicides such as benomyl. Like the systemic insecticides these are taken in by the plants. Leaf spots, such as iris leaf spot, which appear as black or brownish spots on the foliage, should also be controlled by spraying with benomyl fungicide. If ignored, these diseases can seriously affect growth.

Phlox eelworm is a very serious pest of *Phlox paniculata* and it causes deformed, stunted growth — the stems and leaves are affected. It is a microscopic pest and there is no cure except to dig up and burn affected plants. The plants could be propagated from root cuttings as the pest rarely affects the roots.

Dead heads and stems

Dead heading, or the removal of dead flower heads, should be a regular task in the spring, summer and autumn and often it encourages the plants to go on flowering over a longer period. Any plants which produce attractive seed heads, however, should not be dead headed.

In the autumn, when the stems of herbaceous plants have died down, cut down the stems as close to the crowns of the plants as possible, to make sure the beds and borders look neat and tidy. Some people prefer to wait until the spring before cutting down the dead stems as they maintain that the stems afford some frost protection for the plants, but I am not convinced of this; and anyway they become decidedly tatty over the winter. Regular removal of dead leaves from evergreen perennials will help to keep the beds and borders looking tidy and will also help to reduce trouble from pests and diseases.

Division of plants

The majority of perennials need lifting and dividing every three or four years to keep them young and vigorous and free flowering. There are, of course, some, such as paeonias and kniphofias, which do not like disturbance and will thrive for a great many years if left undisturbed. Asters, on the other hand, flower very much better if they are divided every year. They can be split into virtually rooted cuttings, single shoots with a piece of rhizome and a few roots, which can then be planted about 5cm apart each way in bold groups.

There are some perennials which cannot be divided because they come from a tap root, and a good example here is gypsophila. The short-lived perennials, such as *Lychnis coronaria* and lupinus, also cannot be divided and new plants have to be produced from seeds, cuttings or some other suitable method of propagation.

I prefer to lift and divide perennials in the early spring just as they are coming into growth, wherever this is possible. But there are some, such as paeonias, which are best divided in autumn. Spring is certainly best if you have a heavy soil which is inclined to lie wet and cold over the winter. Newly divided plants could rot in such conditions. But if you have a very light well-drained soil then autumn division can be successful. Plants which flower in the early spring, such as *Primula denticulata* and epimediums, should be divided immediately after flowering. The German or flag irises flower in June and these should be divided immediately flowering is over.

Clumps for division should be lifted with a fork and as much soil as possible shaken from the roots. Very large or tough clumps can be split with two garden forks. Thrust the two forks back to back through the centre of the clump and then prise the handles apart — this will result in splitting the plant in two. Repeat the process as many times as necessary until you have divisions of a suitable size for replanting — divisions which sit comfortably in the palm of your hand are generally of adequate size. Remember to discard the centre portion of each clump as this is the oldest part and will be declining in vigour. Save only the young vigorous outer parts of a clump for replanting. When dividing German or flag irises, remember that each division should consist of a fan of leaves and a portion of the swollen rhizome with some roots attached. Replant irises so that the top of the rhizome just shows above the soil surface. If the rhizome is damaged during division dust the wound with a little captan powder to prevent the possibility of rhizome rot.

When the plants have been lifted take the opportunity to thoroughly dig and manure the bed or border before replanting. In the meantime make sure the roots of the plants do not dry out — cover them with polythene sheeting, wet hessian or something similar. Replant the divisions as mentioned under Planting techniques.

Index